Dutch Oven Recipes For One-Pot Meals

Fallon .A Baxter

All rights reserved. Copyright © 2023 Fallon .A Baxter

COPYRIGHT © 2023 Fallon .A Baxter

All rights reserved.

No part of this book must be reproduced, stored in a retrieval system, or shared by any means, electronic, mechanical, photocopying, recording, or otherwise, without written permission from the publisher.

Every precaution has been taken in the preparation of this book; still the publisher and author assume no responsibility for errors or omissions. Nor do they assume any liability for damages resulting from the use of the information contained herein.

Legal Notice:

This book is copyright protected and is only meant for your individual use. You are not allowed to amend, distribute, sell, use, quote or paraphrase any of its part without the written consent of the author or publisher.

Introduction

This is a versatile and comprehensive collection of recipes designed for the contemporary kitchen, showcasing the incredible versatility of the Dutch oven as a cooking tool. This cookbook is a treasure trove of culinary inspiration, spanning various meal categories and culinary traditions.

The cookbook kicks off with an introduction that highlights the Dutch oven's role as the "everyday pot for everything." It emphasizes the Dutch oven's ability to handle a wide range of cooking techniques, making it an indispensable kitchen companion.

The breakfast and brunch section offers an array of morning delights, allowing readers to start their day with delicious dishes prepared in their Dutch ovens. From hearty breakfast casseroles to savory brunch options, this section has something to satisfy every palate.

Moving on to soups, stews, and chilis, the cookbook provides a collection of recipes that showcase the Dutch oven's prowess in slow-cooked comfort foods. Whether you're in the mood for a hearty stew, a comforting soup, or a spicy chili, these recipes offer a delightful range of options.

For seafood enthusiasts, the fish and shellfish section presents mouthwatering recipes that make the most of the Dutch oven's versatility. From succulent seafood stews to flavorful baked fish dishes, these recipes ensure that seafood lovers won't be disappointed.

The poultry section takes center stage with a variety of chicken and turkey recipes. Whether you prefer classic roasted chicken or innovative poultry-based creations, this section offers a diverse selection of Dutch oven delights.

The cookbook then delves into the realm of pork, beef, and lamb, showcasing recipes that celebrate the rich flavors of these meats. From braised pork to tender beef roasts, these dishes are sure to please carnivores.

For those seeking meatless options, the meatless mains section offers a range of plant-based recipes that are both hearty and satisfying. These dishes highlight the Dutch oven's ability to coax maximum flavor from vegetarian ingredients.

The breads and rolls section provides readers with a chance to explore the world of Dutch oven baking. From rustic artisan loaves to fluffy dinner rolls, these recipes demonstrate how the Dutch oven can produce bakery-quality bread at home.

Finally, the desserts section indulges the sweet tooth with delectable treats that can be created in a Dutch oven. From fruity cobblers to decadent chocolate delights, these desserts are the perfect way to conclude a meal.

In summary, this book is a culinary journey that celebrates the Dutch oven's versatility and timeless appeal. With a diverse range of recipes spanning breakfast, brunch, soups, seafood, poultry, meats, meatless mains, bread, and desserts, this cookbook is a valuable resource for anyone looking to elevate their cooking skills and explore the full potential of this iconic kitchen tool. Whether you're a seasoned chef or a novice cook, this cookbook offers something for everyone to enjoy and savor.

Contents

THE EVERYDAY POT FOR EVERYTHING 1
BREAKFAST & BRUNCH 17
    COUNTRY FAIR OMELET 21
    BAKED EGGS WITH CREAMY POLENTA 23
    PB&J POCKETS 25
    BREAKFAST RATATOUILLE WITH CHORIZO, EGGS & CHEESE 27
    HAM & POTATOES AU GRATIN 29
    SCRAMBLED BREAKFAST HASH 31
    FRUIT-TOPPED WAFFLES 33
    BREAKFAST LASAGNA 35
    CHEESE & POTATO SOUFFLÉ 37
    PUMPKIN BLUEBERRY BREAD 39
    CRUSTLESS CHEESE & VEGETABLE QUICHE 41
    HAM, CHEESE & POTATO BAKE 43
    ZUCCHINI GRUYÈRE FRITTATA 45
    SWEET CORNBREAD WITH RAISINS 47
SOUPS, STEWS & CHILIS 51
    POTATO, LEEK & GARBANZO BEAN SOUP 55
    BUTTERNUT SQUASH SOUP 57
    SWEET POTATO BISQUE 59
    SHRIMP & CORN CHOWDER 61
    CREAMY BEET SOUP 63
    CHILLED CARROT SOUP 65
    HEARTY BEEF STEW 67
    BEEF & ROOT VEGETABLE STEW 69
    FRENCH BEEF STEW 71
    SPANISH LAMB STEW 73
    CHICKEN & VEGETABLE STEW 75
    TUSCAN PORK STEW 77
    TURKEY, BEAN & CORN CHILI 79

- SMOKIN' BEEF CHILI 81
- FISH & SHELLFISH 85
  - SPICE-RUBBED SALMON 88
  - STEAMED MUSSELS WITH BACON 90
  - SPANISH PAELLA 92
  - LEMON-GRILLED HALIBUT 94
  - GRILLED SWORDFISH STEAKS 96
  - LINGUINE WITH CLAMS 98
  - SALMON WITH SPINACH 100
  - GROUPER WITH VEGETABLES 102
  - BOUILLABAISSE 104
- POULTRY 108
  - HERBED CHICKEN WITH SPRING VEGETABLES 111
  - RICE WITH CHICKEN & CHORIZO 113
  - AROMATIC CHICKEN POT 115
  - CHICKEN & VEGETABLE STIR-FRY 117
  - CHICKEN WITH ONIONS & GARLIC 119
  - DUCK WITH OLIVE SAUCE 121
  - CHICKEN PASTA BAKE 123
  - LEMON ROAST CHICKEN 125
  - GOAT CHEESE–STUFFED CHICKEN BREASTS 127
  - CHICKEN, POTATO & BROCCOLI CASSEROLE 129
- PORK, BEEF & LAMB 133
  - SPICY PORK WITH WINTER VEGETABLES 137
  - JERK PORK CHOPS WITH PLANTAINS 139
  - SHREDDED PORK BURRITOS 141
  - THREE-WAY PORK POT 143
  - PORK GOULASH 146
  - ROASTED PORK SHOULDER 148
  - PORK WITH RICE & BEANS 150
  - CAJUN RIBLETS 152
  - PORK RIB CASSEROLE 154
  - BEEF BOURGUIGNON 156

- HERB-CRUSTED ROAST BEEF & POTATOES 159
- BEEF TENDERLOIN 161
- BRAISED SHORT RIBS 163
- ROAST BEEF WITH ROOT VEGETABLES 165
- STUFFED MEATBALLS 167
- LAMB SHANKS WITH VEGETABLES 169
- SHEPHERD'S PIE 171
- LAMB CURRY 173
- BRAISED ROSEMARY LAMB SHANKS 175

MEATLESS MAINS 179
- MEDITERRANEAN CHEESE TART 183
- BUTTERNUT SQUASH RISOTTO 185
- MUSHROOM RISOTTO 187
- PUTTANESCA PASTA BAKE 189
- VEGETABLE STIR-FRY 191
- EGGS PIPÉRADE 193
- WARM FARRO SALAD 195
- KALE & SQUASH LASAGNA 197
- VEGETABLE POLENTA CASSEROLE 199
- WILD MUSHROOM PASTA BAKE 201
- RUSTIC PIZZA 203
- CHEESE FONDUE 205
- SQUASH CASSEROLE 207
- MEDLEY OF MUSHROOM STROGANOFF 209
- GREEN BEAN CASSEROLE 211

BREADS & ROLLS 215
- IRISH SODA BREAD 218
- SAVORY CORNBREAD 220
- PARMESAN OLIVE BREAD 222
- IRISH SODA BREAD WITH ROSEMARY & GARLIC 224
- PARMESAN ROSEMARY BREAD 226
- JALAPEÑO CORNBREAD 228
- LEMON BREAD 230

- COCONUT BREAD 232
- SEEDED DINNER ROLLS 234

DESSERTS 238
- CHERRY & ALMOND CRUMBLE 241
- CHOCOLATE BREAD PUDDING 243
- PEAR CRISP 245
- BRANDY BANANA FLAMBÉ 247
- BAKED APPLES WITH CARAMEL SAUCE 249
- ALMOND CAKE 251
- MIXED BERRY BAKE 253
- PEAR & CRANBERRY CRUMBLE 255
- CLASSIC BREAD PUDDING 257
- WHITE WINE & SPICE POACHED PEARS 259
- APPENDIX A 262
- APPENDIX B 264

CHAPTER 1
THE EVERYDAY POT FOR EVERYTHING

The modern Dutch oven (also known as a cocotte, casserole, or French oven) is still made of cast iron and comes in two varieties: plain and enameled. It has earned its place as a kitchen essential, ideal for cooking just about anything, from braises, stews and pot roasts to casseroles, homemade breads and sweet treats. There is no task too big or small for your Dutch oven.

The less expensive option, a plain cast iron oven, will need to be seasoned with oil before initial use to prevent rusting and corrosion, and to ensure that it doesn't react with acidic ingredients, such as tomatoes or wine. Enameled cast iron pots, on the other hand, come ready to use, thanks to an enamel glaze baked on at a high heat (between 1200°F and 1400°F) until it forms a smooth porcelain surface bonded to the iron. Though more expensive, enameled pots are by far the more popular choice. This is not only because they don't require seasoning but also because of their appealing look and finish—and the fact that the naturally nonstick enamel is easier to clean. However, some modern cast-iron manufacturers have introduced lines of pre-seasoned pots, and these are gaining in popularity. All are marvelous options. And who knows—there might be an old Dutch oven in your family's basement, just waiting to be used once again.

Some aluminum and stainless options are available as well. But although considerably cheaper, they don't offer nearly the same ability to retain and release heat evenly across the cooking surface, which is what keeps the food on the bottom of the pot from burning during the slow, steady cooking process synonymous with Dutch ovens.

Size Matters

Dutch ovens range in size from 2 to 12 quarts, the average being 5½ quarts, for which the recipes in this book are designed. Neither too big nor too small, the 5½-quart pot can accommodate a whole chicken, pork loin, boneless pork shoulder, a bunch of short ribs, or lamb shanks. It's large enough to feed a family of four to six—without being too heavy to lift!

Shopping for an Oven

When shopping for a Dutch oven, invest in the best one you can afford. Pots range in price from $50 to $300 or more for a coveted Le Creuset. The price you pay will reflect the quality of your Dutch oven. Whatever your price point, here are some features on which you shouldn't compromise:

- The oven should feel heavy when you hold it, with uniformly thick, solid sides and an equally thick bottom.
- The handles and knob should be sturdy, firmly attached, and oven-safe, and you should be able to grasp them when wearing heavy oven mitts.
- The lid should fit properly, so moisture won't be able to escape.

Money-Saving Tips

There are ways to make your dollars stretch a little further. Given that your Dutch oven will last a lifetime—and possibly the lifetimes of your grandchildren—it's worth spending a little extra time searching out the best value for your budget.

> **SHOP FOR SECONDS:** Le Creuset offers big markdowns on seconds—pots with small flaws but that are otherwise perfect. These can be found at Le Creuset outlet stores or, occasionally, at Marshalls or T. J. Maxx. Other ways to get a great deal include eBay, browsing secondhand shops, and vintage kitchenware stores.

> **LOOK FOR DISCONTINUED COLORS:** Bargains can often be found on Le Creuset pots at local kitchen stores when they're discontinuing one color in order to create more space on shelves for a trendy new hue.

> **CHECK OUT OTHER BRANDS:** Although Le Creuset is considered the Rolls-Royce of Dutch ovens, other brands worth investigating include Lodge, Staub, Tramontina, and Innova, as well as offerings by celebrity chefs Martha Stewart, Mario Batali, and Guy Fieri, which are sometimes co-branded with major department stores. Target and Lodge both sell new, pre-seasoned non-enameled cast-iron Dutch ovens, and vintage brands to look out for include Wagner and Griswold.

ENAMELED DUTCH OVEN MAINTENANCE

With proper care, an enameled cast iron Dutch oven will last a lifetime. Here's how to maintain the integrity and the luster of yours indefinitely.

- Although many Dutch ovens are dishwasher-safe, constant dishwashing may lead to some dulling of the enamel finish. Although this won't harm your cookware, wash yours by hand in warm, soapy water if you wish to preserve the patina.

- Always allow your cookware to cool before washing. Although the enamel coating is extremely durable, you don't want to risk causing thermal shock by plunging a hot pot into cold water.

- For light stains, rub with a dampened cloth and baking soda.

- For more persistent stains, fill the pot with warm water and let it soak for 15 to 20 minutes before washing.

- For stubborn, baked-on food residue, you may have to soak the pot overnight. Then, use a nylon or soft abrasive pad or brush to remove stains. Avoid using scourers, metallic pads, or harsh abrasive cleansing agents, which might scratch or chip the enamel.

- Never store your Dutch oven while still damp.

- Avoid stacking your cookware. If unavoidable, use rubber bumpers (often included in the packing materials) to protect the interior.

- Periodically check handles and knobs, and if anything feels loose, tighten the screws. Food particles sometimes hide in the crevice between the handle and the lid, so occasionally take these parts off and clean any residue you find.

- Although a Dutch oven is extremely durable, the porcelain finish may be damaged if the pot is banged or dropped on a hard surface or floor. In such an instance, the pot won't be covered by your lifetime warranty. Always handle your cookware with care and respect.

Cast Iron Dutch Oven Maintenance Tips

If your cast iron Dutch oven isn't preseasoned, you'll need to season it before first use. This is a process that involves removing the wax applied at the factory to keep your pot rust-free, washing it thoroughly in hot soapy water, and then saturating the pot and lid with oil, and allowing it to bake in a preheated oven for an hour. This seasoning process is necessary to prevent any corrosion, rusting, or reaction with acidic foods. Once this procedure is complete, use boiling water and a brush to remove stains after use. Try to avoid using dish soap. If unavoidable, use a small quantity of a mild formula. Once dry, rub with a thin coating of oil, and store in a clean, dry location with the lid ajar to allow for air to circulate. Otherwise, the oil may leave an unpleasant smell and taste. Placing a paper towel or piece of newspaper inside the oven will absorb any excess moisture.

PERFECT ONE-POT MEALS

The Dutch oven is one of your kitchen's most useful tools. A good Dutch oven goes from the stove top to the oven with ease. With it, you can cook virtually anything in a single pot, from soups and stews to amazing breakfast casseroles, and even desserts. That's why every recipe in this book is cooked in your Dutch oven and only your Dutch oven. With just a single pot, you can make a wide array of delicious foods to keep the whole family happy.

Here are a few reasons why your Dutch oven is the perfect tool for one-pot meals.

IT HAS A LARGE CAPACITY. Depending on the size and brand, a Dutch oven may have a capacity from about 2½ quarts to up to 12 quarts or higher. This can accommodate a lot of food, which makes it perfect for making a one-pot meal and adaptable for a variety of different household sizes.

IT GOES FROM THE STOVE TOP TO THE OVEN. Most Dutch ovens are made with heatproof fittings, so you can start a meal on the stove top and finish it in the oven. This is the perfect way to cook stews and braises.

IT SAVES TIME AND CLEANUP. If you're making an entire meal in a Dutch oven, you don't have a whole bunch of pots and pans to wash after dinner. Likewise, one-pot meals tend to be easier to make, requiring the same cooking method for all ingredients. That saves you time and effort.

DUTCH OVENS COME IN AN ARRAY OF FINISHES TO FIT YOUR NEEDS AND BUDGET. You can find Dutch ovens in an array of materials, such as cast iron, enameled cast iron, and anodized aluminum. Each type has different price points, from very inexpensive to extremely costly. With such a variety of choices and materials, you can find a Dutch oven that works perfectly for you and your family.

THE WEIGHT OF THE DUTCH OVEN ALLOWS FOR EVEN BROWNING. The casting process in making the Dutch oven gives it a heft and weight that transfers heat effectively and evenly. Therefore, it allows you to get a beautiful brown on meats and vegetables that adds flavor to the dish you cook.

DUTCH OVENS ALLOW YOU TO BUILD FLAVORS. When you make a one-pot meal in the Dutch oven, you build flavors. When you cook meats and vegetables, they react to the heat, leaving caramelized brown bits in the bottom of the pan. Adding a little liquid and scraping up the browned bits with the side of a spoon ensures the flavoring from caramelized proteins and sugars goes into your meal instead of remaining on the bottom of the pan.

YOU CAN COOK AT MULTIPLE TEMPERATURES FOR A SINGLE DISH. Many one-pot meals call for a quick sear of meat and vegetables followed by a slow braise with liquids. The Dutch oven is ideally suited to this task.

Because of how evenly it holds heat, you can quickly sear the meat and then turn it down for a long slow braise on the stove top or in the oven.

IT'S EXTREMELY VERSATILE. Along with cooking soups, stews, and other one-pot meals, you can also use your Dutch oven for large capacity, high heat tasks such as boiling pasta or rice. It serves as a workhorse in your kitchen.

COOKING WITH A DUTCH OVEN

PREPARE FOR FIRST USE: Remove all packaging and labels. If your Dutch oven comes with rubber bumpers, set them aside to protect your pot during storage. Wash the pot and lid in hot, soapy water, then rinse and dry thoroughly. Your Dutch oven is now ready to tackle your most demanding one-pot recipes! (Note: If your Dutch oven is non-enameled, follow the seasoning instructions here before first use.)

CHOOSE THE RIGHT UTENSILS: To protect an enamel finish, use silicone, nylon, wooden, or heat-resistant plastic tools. If you must use metal tools, spoons, or whisks, take care not to scrape them over the enamel surface or tap them on the rim. Avoid using handheld electric or battery operated beaters, as their blades will damage the enamel. And never use knives or utensils with sharp edges to cut foods inside the oven.

KNOW YOUR WORK ZONE: Cast iron cookware is suitable for use with all heat sources, including gas, electric, ceramic, and induction cook-tops, and ovens fueled by gas, oil, coal, or wood. When cooking with your Dutch oven on a stove top, always use the burner nearest in size to the diameter of your pot bottom. This will maximize efficiency and prevent hot spots or overheating the pot sides and handles. When using a ceramic, glass-topped stove, always lift the pot when moving it; attempts to slide it across the surface may damage the stove top or the base of the pot. Also, never use your pot in microwave ovens, on outdoor grills, or over campfires (unless it's a special camp oven).

HEAT SLOWLY AND GRADUALLY—MOST OF THE TIME: As a rule, medium or low heat will provide the best results for cooking, including techniques such as frying or searing. Cast iron has a unique and superior ability to distribute and retain heat evenly throughout the vessel—the bottom, the sidewalls, and even the lid. Because cast iron needs less energy to maintain a required temperature, lower the heat accordingly. If you don't, overheating will cause food to stick or burn. A high heat setting should be used only to boil water for vegetables or pasta (never allow your oven to boil dry, as this may permanently damage the enamel), or to reduce the consistency of broths, stocks, or sauces.

GET READY TO GET CREATIVE: The heat retention of cast iron combined with the benefits of porcelain means you can use many cooking techniques with your Dutch oven, including sautéing, frying, searing, braising, stewing, roasting, broiling, and baking. Because the porcelain enamel is resistant to acidic and alkaline foods, the pot can even be used to marinate and refrigerate foods.

COOKING IN THE OVEN: Check the maximum oven temperature recommended for the hardware on your cookware. Pots with cast iron or stainless steel handles and knobs can be used at any oven temperature, but the heat-resistant temperature of knobs made of phenolic materials (types of plastic or resin engineered to withstand high temperatures) can fall in the range of 375°F to 480°F. Pots with wooden handles or knobs should not be placed in the oven. Also be careful of ovens with cast iron linings—placing cast iron cookware on the floor will result in an increased cooking rate inside your Dutch oven, causing food to overcook. For best results, always place the pot on a shelf or rack.

COOKING ON THE GRILL: The only exception to the "heat food slowly" rule is when grilling or caramelizing. For this, you'll need to achieve a hot surface temperature before you begin, rather than low or medium, as you would to cook food slowly. In this case, place the empty pot on a medium setting, and allow it to heat for several minutes. Don't add oil—it may become too hot and smoke. Dip your fingers in water, and scatter a few drops over the surface of your pot. If they sizzle and evaporate immediately, the pot is hot enough to use. At this point, you can lightly oil it with a vegetable oil, a nut oil, or corn oil (rather than olive oil, which may cause excessive smoking).

FRYING AND SAUTÉING: Because the fat will need to be hot before adding food, bring the pot and oil to the correct temperature together. You'll know the oil is hot enough when there's a slight ripple in the surface. For butter and other fats, look for the moment it starts bubbling or foaming. If the fat begins smoking, it's too hot. In this case, remove the pot from the heat source for a few moments.

DEEP-FRYING: Keep the pot no more than one-third full of oil to allow enough room for the oil level to rise once foods are added. Keep the lid close by in case the oil overheats. For added safety, use an oilfrying thermometer, and never leave the pot unattended.

HANDLE WITH CARE: Always use oven mitts to protect hands from hot cookware, handles, or knobs. Protect your countertops and table by placing your Dutch oven on a wooden board, silicone mat, trivet, or a dry, heavy folded cloth.

STOCKING YOUR PANTRY

The secret to whipping up delicious home-cooked meals in a flash—sans last-minute trips to the grocery store—is having a well-stocked pantry. In addition to your classic perishables—bread, milk, eggs, and meat—these perennial stalwarts will ensure you're never short of great ingredients.

BROTH OR STOCK: The addition of broth or stock is a simple trick for delivering a flavorful punch to soups, sauces, gravies, and casseroles. You can also use either one in place of water to add a salty kick to simple side dishes, such as rice. Keep a variety of chicken, beef, and vegetable broths or stocks on hand.

CANNED BEANS: Beloved the world over, beans are inexpensive, easy to prepare, filling, and nutritious (they're a fantastic source of both fiber and protein).

Served as a side to meat and veggies, they taste great on their own, but beans also make an excellent addition to casseroles, pasta dishes, or cold salads. With so many varieties to choose from—including garbanzo, black, pinto, navy, and kidney beans—your family won't ever get bored.

CANNED TOMATOES: Used in everything from casseroles to pasta dishes, you'll never want to be without the versatile tomato. Although nothing beats the taste and smell of one plucked fresh from a summer garden, luckily you can get tomatoes year round in a can. Keep on hand a mix of diced, crushed, and whole tomatoes.

CANNED TUNA: Another multitasking superstar, tuna is much more than a sandwich filling. Stir into pasta, add to a casserole, sprinkle on top of a salad, or mix with avocado for a tempting snack packed with protein and heart-healthy omega-3s.

GARLIC: Slice it, dice it, mince it, crush it, roast it, sauté it, or grill it—garlic is one great little herb, allowing you to add its unique savor to dishes quickly and easily. Stock up on fresh garlic in whole cloves or buy the already peeled and chopped variety to quickly add to soups, stews, sautés, stir-fries, and marinades. Bonus: Garlic is revered as a cure-all that improves digestion, circulation, respiratory health, and fertility!

MARINARA SAUCE: No pantry is complete without a few jars of spaghetti sauce. They provide a great backup for those days you don't have time to make your own sauce. Simply stir into hot cooked pasta, top with freshly grated Parmesan cheese and some fresh basil leaves, and serve.

OIL: Olive, nut, and vegetable oils are essential for cooking, making salad dressings, and drizzling over grilled fish, pasta, and vegetable sides.

PASTA: Boxed pasta is inexpensive, has virtually no expiration date, and can be mixed in with a variety of meals. Whip up a quick and easy main dish in minutes by tossing with spices and grilled steak, shrimp, or chicken; pair with fresh vegetables and herbs; or just add a jar of pasta sauce. Whole-wheat pasta packs more fiber than regular white noodles, so your family will feel fuller, longer.

POTATOES AND ONIONS: These versatile veggies add their own special touch to just about any dish, from soups to stir-fries to frittatas. Never store them in the refrigerator or in plastic bags—they'll do best in the interior of your cool, dark, well-ventilated pantry.

RICE: Another staple beloved the world over, rice makes a great main component of casseroles and stir-fries, or it can serve as a satisfying side dish to complement any meat and vegetable combo. For maximum nutrition, choose less-processed brown rice over standard enriched white rice.

SALT, PEPPER, AND SPICES: Some simple seasonings can take any meal from satisfying to sensational in a flash. Start with the essentials—sea salt and peppercorns—and build from there. Expand your taste buds with dried herbs, such as basil, thyme, oregano, rosemary, and bay leaves.

VINEGAR: With varieties including balsamic, cider, sherry, and wine, incredibly versatile vinegar enlivens certain dishes and many salad dressings. Bonus: Vinegar is also reported to help open up blood vessels and improve blood flow.

Recipe Key

GF Gluten-Free	**V** Vegetarian	**30** 30-Minutes
DF Dairy-Free	**V** Vegan	

Tips for Leftovers

Leftovers? No problem. Save them for another day with these safe storage tips.

- Although modern refrigerators are built to cool hot dishes, it's safer and more energy conscious to allow leftovers to cool a little before placing them in the refrigerator. That said, always store leftovers within two hours of cooking (or one hour on hot summer days).

- Shallow, thin-walled metal, glass, or plastic containers are ideal for storage. Bags, aluminum foil, and plastic wrap work well for larger or awkwardly shaped foods. For foods with a pungent smell, foil creates a stronger barrier to retain odors. Acidic foods, such as tomatoes and berries, should always be wrapped in plastic; the acids will react with the aluminum in foil, leaving a harmless but unsightly blue residue. An enameled cast iron Dutch oven can be used to keep foods cold. The vitreous enamel surface is impermeable and therefore ideal for food storage. Pull out your chilled dish the following day in an attractive, table-ready cold food server!

- Cooked meat can be stored three to four days in the refrigerator. Casseroles, veggies, and similar side dishes, as well as pie, will usually last three to five days.

- If you have a considerable amount of leftovers, consider freezing them. Freezing completely halts bacterial activity, so food can stay safe and usable for three to six months. Any longer and your leftovers will start to lose nutritional value and quality; frozen cooked meats will begin to lose their savor after three months.

- It's a good idea to wrap a snug layer of foil around plastic-wrapped foods before freezing, because the foil keeps out oxygen, which causes freezer burn.

- Your Dutch oven can also be placed in the freezer for food storage—though it's unlikely you'll want to be without it that long!

- Non-enameled pots are great for cooking but avoid putting them in the fridge or freezer—they may react with foods or rust.

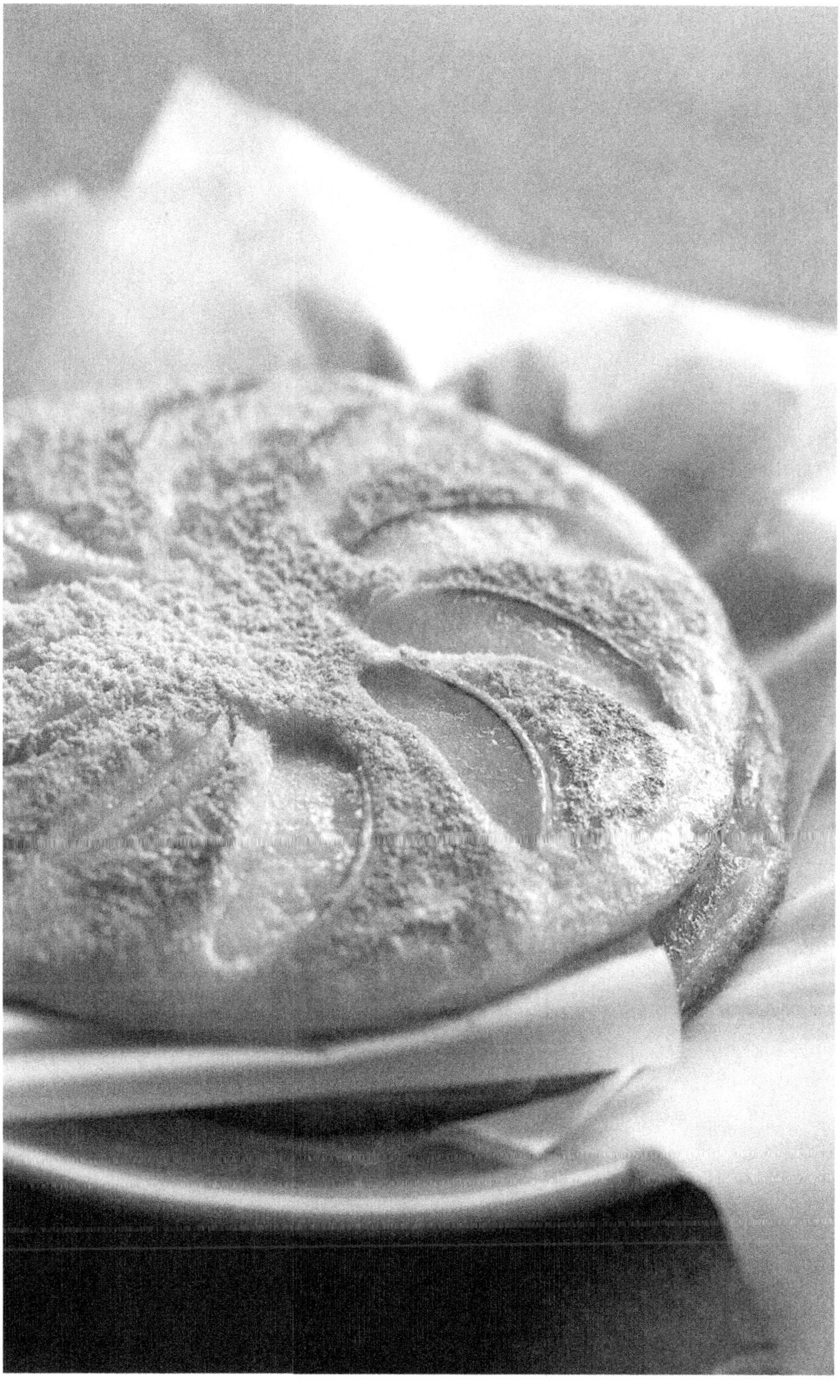

CHAPTER 2
BREAKFAST & BRUNCH

APPLE PANCAKE

COUNTRY FAIR OMELET

BAKED EGGS WITH CREAMY POLENTA

PB&J POCKETS

BREAKFAST RATATOUILLE WITH CHORIZO, EGGS & CHEESE

HAM & POTATOES AU GRATIN

SCRAMBLED BREAKFAST HASH

FRUIT-TOPPED WAFFLES

BREAKFAST LASAGNA

CHEESE & POTATO SOUFFLE

PUMPKIN BLUEBERRY BREAD

CRUSTLESS CHEESE & VEGETABLE QUICHE

HAM, CHEESE & POTATO BAKE

ZUCCHINI GRUYERE FRITTATA

SWEET CORNBREAD WITH RAISINS

APPLE PANCAKE

SERVES 4 TO 6 PREP TIME: 10 MINUTES COOK TIME: 30 MINUTES

Who doesn't love waking up to the aroma of a freshly cooked pancake? Add some apple, nutmeg, and cinnamon, and this Saturday morning stalwart is transformed into a sumptuous, mouthwatering treat.

V | 30

4 eggs
½ cup unbleached all-purpose flour
½ teaspoon baking powder
1 tablespoon sugar
Pinch salt
1 cup milk
2 tablespoons unsalted butter, melted
1 teaspoon ground nutmeg, divided
½ cup white sugar, divided
½ teaspoon ground cinnamon
4 tablespoons unsalted butter
1 large apple, peeled, cored, and sliced

1 Preheat the oven to 425°F.

2 In a large bowl, blend the eggs, flour, baking powder, 1 tablespoon sugar, and salt. Gradually add in the milk, stirring constantly. Add the

melted butter and ½ teaspoon of nutmeg. If possible, let the batter stand for 30 minutes.

3 In a small bowl, combine ¼ cup of sugar, cinnamon, and the remaining ½ teaspoon of nutmeg.

4 Melt the 4 tablespoons butter in a Dutch oven over a medium-high heat.

5 Remove the pot from the stove top. Sprinkle the sugar mixture evenly over the butter, then line the bottom with the apple slices. Sprinkle the remaining ¼ cup of sugar on top.

6 Place the pot back over a medium-high heat. When the mixture begins to bubble, pour the batter evenly over the apples.

7 Cover, place in the preheated oven, and bake for 15 minutes.

8 Reduce heat to 375°F and bake for 10 minutes, or until a toothpick comes out clean.

9 use a plastic spatula to loosen the pancake, slide it onto a serving platter, cut into wedges, and serve.

COOKING TIP: *To add a nice, nutty accent, place 8 to 10 whole pecans around the top of the pancake before placing the pot in the oven.*

COUNTRY FAIR OMELET

SERVES 6 TO 8 PREP TIME: 10 MINUTES COOK TIME: 30 MINUTES

The addition of sausage transforms a light omelet into hearty fare that will satiate the entire family—and keep them energized for all the weekend chores. For a tasty twist, swap in breakfast sausage made with a blend of pork and beef, or try chicken links for a lighter, healthier option.

GF 30

2 tablespoons olive, coconut, or canola oil, or cooking spray
½ pound breakfast sausage, cut crosswise into 1/4-inch-thick slices
½ pound bacon, thickly sliced
½ onion, diced
1 clove garlic, minced
1 red bell pepper, seeded and chopped
1 cup mushrooms, chopped
9 eggs
½ cup milk
1 cup grated Cheddar cheese
Salt
Freshly ground black pepper

---

1 Preheat the oven to 375°F.

2 Heat a Dutch oven over medium heat. Add the oil or a spritz of cooking spray, and fry the sausage until browned, then remove and set aside on a plate, using a paper towel to absorb any excess fat.

3 Fry the bacon until browned, and drain excess fat from the Dutch oven.

4 Add the sausage, onion, garlic, pepper, and mushrooms. Sauté until the vegetables are tender.

5 In a bowl, mix the eggs and milk, then pour the egg mixture into the pot.

6 Cover, place in the heated oven, and bake for 20 minutes, or until the eggs are firm.

7 Sprinkle cheese on top, and season with salt and pepper. Return the pot to the oven for a few minutes, uncovered, until the cheese melts. Serve.

> **COOKING TIP:** *To add a zesty Southwestern kick, top the omelet with salsa—your choice of mild, medium, or hot.*

BAKED EGGS WITH CREAMY POLENTA

SERVES 4 TO 6 PREP TIME: 5 MINUTES COOK TIME: 45 MINUTES

With minimal prep time, this is the perfect brunch to whip together when entertaining overnight guests. Let the hard-working Dutch oven do most of the work while you sit back and catch up with friends and family over a hot cup of joe.

GF **V**

Cooking spray

½ cup instant polenta

1 cup water

1 cup milk

½ cup finely grated pecorino romano cheese

Pinch salt

Pinch freshly ground black pepper

4 eggs

1 Preheat the oven to 375°F.

2 Generously coat a Dutch oven with cooking spray. Add the polenta, water, milk, cheese, salt, and pepper. Stir.

3 Cover, place in the heated oven, and bake for 30 to 35 minutes, stirring once halfway through, until polenta is tender.

4 use the back of a spoon to make four deep wells in the polenta, then crack an egg into each well. Cover the pot and bake for 10 to 12 minutes, or until the egg whites are cooked.

> **SUBSTITUTION TIP:** *No polenta? No problem! You can substitute cornmeal. Looking for more options? If you prefer your eggs a little firmer, bake for an extra few minutes. For a jolt of delectability, serve with a spoonful of pesto.*

PB&J POCKETS

MAKES 2 POCKETS PREP TIME: 10 MINUTES COOK TIME: 6 MINUTES

This is a delicious Dutch oven take on the classic PB&J. Sure to satisfy kids of all ages, this recipe provides the perfect indoor activity to entertain the troops on a rain-soaked Sunday morning. They'll love rolling up their sleeves and joining in the prep work!

V **30**

FOR THE POCKETS

2 slices 1-inch-thick white bread

2 tablespoons peanut butter

2 tablespoons jam (choice of strawberry, raspberry, blackberry, or blueberry)

2 eggs, lightly beaten

2 tablespoons milk

1 teaspoon maple syrup

¼ teaspoon vanilla extract

Pinch nutmeg

Extra-virgin olive oil

FOR THE TOPPINGS

Your choice of crème fraîche, honey, fresh berries, or pancake syrup

1 Warm a Dutch oven over a low heat.

2 Use a serrated knife to carefully cut horizontally through each slice of bread to within ¼ inch of the bottom crust, creating a pocket. Be careful not to cut through the crust.

3 Spread a layer of peanut butter and a layer of jam in each pocket, and set the bread aside.

4 In a medium bowl, combine the eggs, milk, maple syrup, vanilla extract, and nutmeg, and whisk until well combined.

5 Lightly oil the Dutch oven. Dip a slice of stuffed bread into the egg batter, covering both sides. Place the bread into the Dutch oven and fry for 2 to 3 minutes, or until golden brown. Turn the bread over and fry the other side. Repeat as needed.

6 Serve 2 slices with a choice of toppings.

> **COOKING TIP:** *The beauty of this dish is you can make as much or as little as you like. Big crowd? Make a big bowl of batter, and keep stuffing and frying until everyone's been served.*

BREAKFAST RATATOUILLE WITH CHORIZO, EGGS & CHEESE

SERVES 4 TO 6 PREP TIME: 10 MINUTES COOK TIME: 50 MINUTES

Though it's intended here as part of a breakfast dish, the simple but tasty vegetable and chorizo sauce is extremely versatile—make extra and save it for when you need a delicious accompaniment to a pasta dish in a pinch. Store in a large mason jar in the refrigerator or in plastic bags in the freezer.

GF

2 tablespoons extra-virgin olive oil

5½ ounces chorizo, diced

2 red onions, chopped

3 garlic cloves, minced

1 zucchini, diced

1½ pounds portobello mushrooms

2 red bell peppers, seeded and diced

1 (15-ounce) can chopped tomatoes

2 tablespoons white wine vinegar

1¼ cups water, plus more if necessary

1 teaspoon sugar

Salt

Freshly ground black pepper

4 eggs

5 ounces Parmesan cheese, grated

1 Preheat the oven to 400°F.

2 Heat the olive oil in a Dutch oven over medium heat. Add the chorizo, onions, and garlic, and cook for 4 to 5 minutes.

3 Add the zucchini, mushrooms, and peppers, and cook for 2 to 3 minutes, stirring occasionally.

4 Add the can of tomatoes, stir in the vinegar, water, and sugar, and season with salt and pepper. Bring to a full boil, then reduce heat to a low simmer. Cook for 25 to 30 minutes, stirring occasionally. If the sauce becomes too thick, add more water.

5 Make 4 deep wells in the mixture with the back of a spoon. Crack an egg into each well. Sprinkle cheese on top. Bake for 10 to 12 minutes, or until the sauce is bubbling and the eggs have set.

> **SUBSTITUTION TIP:** *Vegetarian? Substitute vegetables, such as eggplant or squash, in place of the chorizo for an appetizing meatless variation of this creative breakfast dish.*

HAM & POTATOES AU GRATIN

SERVES 4 TO 6 PREP TIME: 5 MINUTES COOK TIME: 30 MINUTES

If you end up with leftovers, serve this au gratin dish for a delicious teatime treat. It makes a satisfying savory topping on a thick wedge of Texas toast.

30

4 tablespoons butter
1 onion, minced
2 cups milk
3 tablespoons flour
1½ cups diced cooked ham
3 cups diced potatoes
Salt
Freshly ground black pepper
½ cup grated Cheddar cheese

1 Preheat the oven to 400°F.

2 Melt the butter in a Dutch oven over medium heat. Sauté the onion, add the milk, and stir.

3 Gradually blend in the flour, stirring constantly, until the mixture thickens.

4 Add the ham and potatoes, and mix well. Season with salt and pepper, and sprinkle the cheese on top.

5 Cover, place in the heated oven, and bake for 20 minutes.

SCRAMBLED BREAKFAST HASH

SERVES 6 PREP TIME: 10 MINUTES COOK TIME: 2 ½ HOURS

This decadent dish makes a fantastic post-holiday breakfast. In place of the sausages called for here, simply use the leftover meat from your celebrations in this delicious hash. Try ham, turkey, kielbasa, brisket, or anything else you might have on hand—even baked or smoked salmon. This recipe also works wonderfully well with meat substitutes like seasoned tofu or veggie crumbles.

GF

2 tablespoons extra-virgin olive oil
1 pound breakfast sausages, diced
4 medium Yukon Gold potatoes, chopped
8 ounces mushrooms, sliced
1 onion, chopped
Salt
Freshly ground black pepper
6 eggs
3 tablespoons milk
½ cup shredded cheese (Cheddar or Monterey Jack)
Salsa or hot pepper sauce, for garnish

1 Preheat the oven to 325°F.

2 Heat the olive oil in a Dutch oven over medium-high heat, and cook the sausages until browned. Drain off the fat. Add the potatoes, mushrooms, and onion, season with salt and pepper, and gently stir. Cover, place in the heated oven, and bake for 1½ to 2 hours, or until the potatoes are tender.

3 In a medium bowl, whisk together the eggs and milk. Pour the egg mixture over the potato mixture. Sprinkle the cheese on top. Cover and bake for 10 to 15 minutes, or until the eggs are set and the cheese has melted.

4 Garnish with the salsa or hot pepper sauce.

> **COOKING TIP:** *To switch things up, make this a sunny-side-up hash instead of a scrambled hash by omitting the milk; then instead of whisking the eggs, crack them directly over the potato mixture before sprinkling cheese on top and baking.*

FRUIT-TOPPED WAFFLES

SERVES 8　PREP TIME: 5 MINUTES　COOK TIME: 2 HOURS

The fruit topping is so tasty, its popularity comes as no surprise. Consider making an extra-large batch and freezing half—you'll appreciate it on those days you need to rustle up breakfast in a flash.

V

Extra-virgin olive oil, for greasing

3 pears, cored and cubed

1 (15-ounce) can pineapple chunks, undrained

1 (15-ounce) can pitted red sweet cherries, undrained

1 cup quartered dried apricots

2 tablespoons brown sugar

1 tablespoon cornstarch (or 1½ tablespoons all-purpose flour)

¼ cup chopped and toasted pecans

16 frozen waffles, toasted

1 Preheat the oven to 325°F.

2 In a lightly oiled Dutch oven, combine the pears, pineapple, cherries, apricots, brown sugar, and cornstarch (or flour, if using). Cover, place in the heated oven, and bake for 1½ to 2 hours.

3 In a small pan over medium heat, dry toast the pecans until brown, for 1 to 2 minutes.

4 Drizzle the hot fruit mixture over the freshly toasted waffles, sprinkle with pecans, and serve.

> **INGREDIENT TIP:** *For crispier pecans, lightly fry them in a little extra-virgin olive oil (or your favorite substitute) until light brown, or if your burners are all taken, preheat the oven to 350°F, and bake for 5 to 10 minutes, turning once or twice.*

BREAKFAST LASAGNA

SERVES 6 TO 8 PREP TIME: 10 MINUTES COOK TIME: 2 HOURS

Lasagna is a traditional Italian dish native to the coastal city of Naples. Here, tortillas, salsa verde, and Monterey Jack cheese give it a Southwestern makeover—and a gluten-free twist.

GF

Cooking spray

1 pound breakfast sausage, casings removed

1 green pepper, seeded and chopped

5 eggs, beaten

2 green onions, sliced

¼ cup chopped fresh parsley

½ teaspoon salt

½ teaspoon cumin

9 corn tortillas

2 cups shredded Monterey Jack cheese, divided

1 (8-ounce) jar salsa verde, divided

1 Preheat the oven to 325°F.

2 Lightly coat a Dutch oven with cooking spray. Cook sausage over medium-high heat until browned, using a plastic or wooden spatula to break up the meat as it cooks. Drain off fat. Add the green pepper, stir, and cook for 1 minute. Add eggs and cook over medium heat

until set, stirring to break up the eggs. Add the green onions, parsley, salt, and cumin, and stir. Transfer the sausage mixture to a large bowl.

3 Place 3 of the tortillas in the bottom of the Dutch oven, layering them over each other as needed. Spoon half the sausage mixture on to the tortilla base, sprinkle the mixture with ½ cup of cheese, then pour ⅓ cup salsa verde on top. Top with 3 more tortillas. Add the remaining sausage mixture, sprinkle with another ½ cup of cheese, and pour the remaining ⅔ cup of salsa verde on top. Cover with the remaining 3 tortillas, and sprinkle the remaining 1 cup of cheese on top.

4 Cover and bake for 1½ hours.

> **COOKING TIP:** *Using two spatulas and a bit of coordination, remove the lasagna from the Dutch oven before cutting to avoid damaging the enamel lining with a knife. If desired, garnish with sour cream and sliced green onions before serving.*

CHEESE & POTATO SOUFFLÉ

SERVES 6 TO 8 PREP TIME: 20 MINUTES COOK TIME: 20 MINUTES

A soufflé is a classic omelet that gets lighter by separating and beating the egg whites. But sliced potatoes ensure this special breakfast treat is substantial enough to keep little bellies full. The nonstick surface of the Dutch oven makes it a perfect cooking partner.

GF **V** **30**

2 tablespoons butter

4 shallots, finely chopped

8 new potatoes, cooked and thinly sliced

8 eggs, separated

1 teaspoon Italian seasoning

1 cup grated cheese (Monterey Jack or Cheddar)

Salt

Freshly ground black pepper

1 Preheat the oven to 325°F.

2 Melt the butter in a Dutch oven over medium heat. Add the shallots and sauté until they begin to soften and brown. Layer the potato slices in the pot, and continue cooking until they're hot.

3 In a medium bowl, combine the egg yolks, Italian seasoning, and cheese, salt and pepper, and beat until frothy. In a separate bowl,

beat the egg whites until stiff.

4 Fold about half the whites into the yolk mixture. When fully blended, fold in the remaining egg whites. Pour this mixture into the Dutch oven, and spread it over the potatoes. Cook for 2 to 3 minutes, until lightly browned and the bottom is set. The top should still be wet and runny.

5 Place in the heated oven, uncovered, and bake until the top puffs up and turns a nice golden brown.

PUMPKIN BLUEBERRY BREAD

SERVES 8   PREP TIME: 20 MINUTES   COOK TIME: 1 HOUR

The addition of pumpkin pie spice makes this recipe a fall favorite, but this breakfast bread is great any time of year. For a slightly tart variation, try substituting cranberries for the blueberries. When out of season, use frozen berries.

DF **V**

2 eggs
1 cup canned pumpkin
1 cup sugar
½ cup vegetable oil
2 cups all-purpose flour
1½ teaspoons pumpkin pie spice
1 teaspoon baking soda
½ teaspoon salt
1 cup fresh or frozen blueberries, divided
1 tablespoon all-purpose flour
Cooking spray

1 Preheat the oven to 325°F.

2 In a medium bowl, mix the eggs, pumpkin, sugar, and vegetable oil.

3 In a large bowl, stir together the flour, pumpkin pie spice, baking soda, and salt. Empty the pumpkin mixture into the flour mixture and

stir.

4 In a small bowl, combine the blueberries and the tablespoon of flour, and toss gently. Then gently fold ⅔ cup blueberries into the batter.

5 Spoon the batter into a Dutch oven, lightly coated with cooking spray. Top with the remaining ⅓ cup blueberries.

6 Cover, place in the oven, and bake for about an hour, or until a toothpick comes out clean.

> **COOKING TIP:** *Before removing the bread from the Dutch oven, allow it to cool for about 10 minutes. Then use a wide wooden or plastic spatula to loosen the sides of the bread, and gently empty onto a wire rack to finish cooling.*

CRUSTLESS CHEESE & VEGETABLE QUICHE

SERVES 6 PREP TIME: 30 MINUTES COOK TIME: 1½ HOURS

Delicious in their own right, quiches are also great ways to use up leftovers. Feel free to substitute whatever vegetables or meat (for a non-vegetarian option) you might have remaining after last night's supper.

GF **V**

2 tablespoons extra-virgin olive oil
8 ounces potatoes, diced
1 yellow summer squash, diced
1 red bell pepper, chopped
4 green onions, sliced
6 eggs, lightly beaten
1½ cups milk
2 tablespoons chopped fresh parsley
Salt
Freshly ground black pepper
1½ cups shredded Cheddar cheese, divided
Cooking spray

1 Preheat the oven to 325°F.

2 In a Dutch oven over medium heat, heat the olive oil, and cook the potatoes for 8 to 10 minutes, or until lightly browned.

3 Add the squash and cook for 4 minutes. Stir in the red pepper, and cook for 2 minutes. Stir in the green onions, and remove the Dutch oven from the heat. Transfer the vegetables to a medium bowl.

4 In a large bowl, combine the eggs, milk, and parsley, and season with salt and pepper. Stir in the cooked vegetables and 1 cup of cheese.

5 Lightly coat the Dutch oven with cooking spray, pour in the vegetable mixture, and sprinkle the remaining ½ cup of cheese on top.

6 Cover, place in the heated oven, and bake for about 1½ hours, or until a knife inserted in the center comes out clean.

HAM, CHEESE & POTATO BAKE

SERVES 8   PREP TIME: 10 MINUTES   COOK TIME: 2 HOURS

If you don't have English muffins on hand, use any type of toasted bread. If using large slices of bread, cut in half for adults and into soldiers (thin strips of toast) for children's plates. This dish easily becomes gluten-sensitivity-friendly by substituting gluten-free bread.

Cooking spray
4 cups frozen diced hash brown potatoes
8 ounces cooked ham, chopped
1 cup shredded Muenster cheese
1 red bell pepper, chopped
1 onion, chopped
6 eggs, lightly beaten
1 (15-ounce) can condensed cream of mushroom soup
½ cup milk
Salt
Freshly ground black pepper
8 English muffins, split and toasted

1 Preheat the oven to 325°F.

2 In a Dutch oven coated with cooking spray, combine the potatoes, ham, cheese, red pepper, and onion.

3 In a medium bowl, mix the eggs, soup, and milk. Season with salt and black pepper, then pour the egg mixture over the potato mixture.

4 Cover, place in the heated oven, and bake for 1½ to 2 hours.

5 Serve over freshly toasted English muffins.

> **SUBSTITUTION TIP:** *Some folks aren't fans of hash browns. In that case, just swap in 4 cups of diced potatoes.*

ZUCCHINI GRUYÈRE FRITTATA

SERVES 8 PREP TIME: 20 MINUTES   COOK TIME: 2 HOURS

This savory bread pudding can be adapted a thousand ways, using any combination of bread, eggs, cheese, and vegetables—or meat, for carnivores. It's easy to prepare, filling, and toothsome, making it the perfect Sunday brunch bake.

V

2 tablespoons extra-virgin olive oil

3 zucchini, diced

6 cups Italian flatbread or focaccia, cut into bite-size cubes

2 cups shredded Gruyère cheese

2 tablespoons chopped fresh parsley

1 teaspoon chopped fresh thyme (or ¼ teaspoon dried thyme, crushed)

6 eggs, lightly beaten

2 cups milk

Salt

Freshly ground black pepper

1 Preheat the oven to 325°F.

2 In a Dutch oven over medium-high heat, heat the olive oil until shimmering. Add the zucchini and cook until lightly browned. Transfer the zucchini to a large bowl.

3 Add the bread cubes, Gruyère, parsley, and thyme to the zucchini, and stir together. Spoon the mixture into the Dutch oven.

4 In the same bowl, whisk the eggs and milk together, and season with salt and black pepper. Pour the egg mixture over the bread mixture, making sure that all of the bread is covered.

5 Cover, place in the heated oven, and bake for 2 hours, or until a knife inserted in the center comes out clean.

> **INGREDIENT TIP:** *Although often associated with Italian cooking, zucchini originated in the Americas. Long used in Central and South America—several thousand years, in fact—this green summer squash wasn't introduced to Europe until Christopher Columbus brought back seeds from his transatlantic voyage.*

SWEET CORNBREAD WITH RAISINS

SERVES 8   PREP TIME: 15 MINUTES   COOK TIME: 1 HOUR

What would a Dutch oven cookbook be without a cornbread recipe? A tradition that dates back three hundred years—as long as the cast-iron pot itself—cornbread was the perfect portable and nutritional powerhouse for the early European colonists in North America. This sweet variation claims its place at the center of the modern-day American table.

V

1½ cups flour
½ cup sugar
1 teaspoon cinnamon
¼ teaspoon nutmeg
1 tablespoon baking powder
¼ teaspoon salt
2 tablespoons extra-virgin olive oil
2 cups milk
½ cup cornmeal
2 eggs
2 tablespoons canola oil
½ cup raisins

1 Preheat the oven to 350°F.

2 In a medium bowl, combine the flour, sugar, cinnamon, nutmeg, baking powder, and salt.

3 Lightly coat a Dutch oven with the olive oil, and heat the milk over medium-high heat until it starts to steam. Add the cornmeal, and reduce the heat to a simmer. Stir for about 10 minutes, or until thick.

4 In a small bowl, beat the eggs and canola oil, and stir the mixture into the cornmeal.

5 Stir the flour and sugar mixture into the cornmeal, and then stir in the raisins.

6 Cover, place in the heated oven, and bake for 40 to 60 minutes, or until a toothpick comes out clean.

NUTRITION TIP: *A 1-ounce serving of cornbread contains 1.8 grams of fiber, which not only helps regulate bowel movements but also helps absorb cholesterol and lower blood sugar levels. And because fiber isn't digested but simply passes through the digestive tract, it's filling without piling on the calories.*

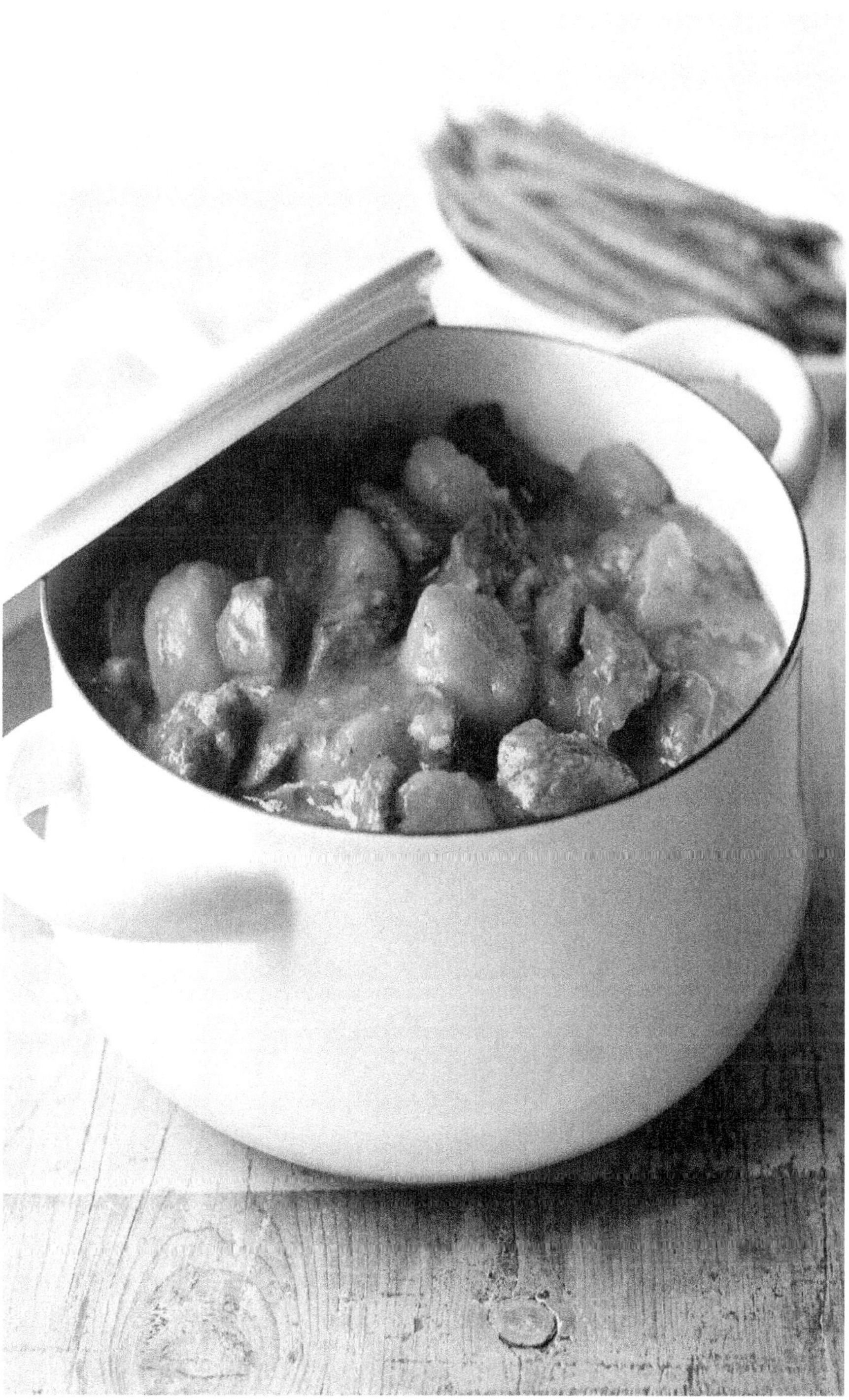

CHAPTER 3
SOUPS, STEWS & CHILIS

CHICKEN NOODLE SOUP

POTATO, LEEK & GARBANZO BEAN SOUP

BUTTERNUT SQUASH SOUP

SWEET POTATO BISQUE

SHRIMP & CORN CHOWDER

CREAMY BEET SOUP

CHILLED CARROT SOUP

HEARTY BEEF STEW

BEEF & ROOT VEGETABLE STEW

FRENCH BEEF STEW

SPANISH LAMB STEW

CHICKEN & VEGETABLE STEW

TUSCAN PORK STEW

TURKEY, BEAN & CORN CHILI
SMOKIN' BEEF CHILI

CHICKEN NOODLE SOUP

SERVES 8 PREP TIME: 20 MINUTES COOK TIME: 1½ TO 2 HOURS

Science has proven what moms have long known: A bowl of chicken soup is good not just for the soul but also for boosting the immune system. Anti-inflammatory properties help dampen cold symptoms while extra electrolytes help you stay hydrated, the key to a speedy recovery.

DF

1 quart chicken broth or stock

3 cups water

2½ cups chopped cooked chicken

3 carrots, sliced

3 stalks celery, sliced

1½ cups sliced mushrooms

¼ cup chopped onion

1½ teaspoons dried thyme, crushed

2 cloves garlic, crushed

Salt

Freshly ground black pepper

2 cups dried egg noodles

1 Preheat the oven to 350°F.

2 In a Dutch oven, combine the broth, water, chicken, carrots, celery, mushrooms, onion, thyme, and garlic, and season with salt and pepper.

3 Cover, place in the heated oven, and bake for 1½ to 2 hours.

4 Stir in the uncooked noodles.

5 Cover and bake for 10 to 15 minutes, or until the noodles are tender.

> **COOKING TIP:** *To boost the goodness of this nourishing soup, add more vegetables. A packet of frozen mixed vegetables makes an easy, quick, and vitamin-rich addition.*

POTATO, LEEK & GARBANZO BEAN SOUP

SERVES 6 TO 8 PREP TIME: 20 MINUTES COOK TIME: 30 MINUTES

This delicious soup packs a powerful nutritional punch. Not only is it rich in vitamins and minerals, it's an antioxidant powerhouse, thanks to the addition of fiber-rich garbanzo beans.

GF | V | 30

- 3 tablespoons butter
- 3 tablespoons extra-virgin olive oil
- 5 to 6 leeks, cleaned and chopped
- 3 cloves garlic, chopped
- 3 to 4 potatoes, cubed
- 2 (15-ounce) cans garbanzo beans, drained
- 3 cups chicken broth or stock
- 1 cup freshly grated Parmesan cheese
- Sea salt
- Freshly ground black pepper

1 In a Dutch oven over medium heat, melt the butter and olive oil. Add the leeks and garlic. Cook for 10 minutes, or until the leeks are translucent.

2 Add the potatoes and garbanzo beans, and cook for 2 to 3 minutes.

3 Add the broth and bring to a boil. Reduce heat and simmer for 20 minutes.

4 Stir in the cheese and season with salt and pepper.

> **COOKING TIP:** *Save some of the leeks, and use as a garnish. Sprinkle with a little extra Parmesan cheese, and drizzle with a dash of olive oil.*

BUTTERNUT SQUASH SOUP

SERVES 6 TO 8 PREP TIME: 20 MINUTES COOK TIME: 1½ HOURS

The best thing about cooking soup in a Dutch oven is that the pot doubles as a handsome serving dish. Simply transfer the Dutch oven from stove to table, and place on a trivet or folded dish towel.

GF

4 tablespoons butter
1 onion, chopped
2 cups chopped carrots
4 cups chopped butternut squash
1 cup peeled and chopped sweet potato
4 cups chicken broth or stock
1 cup heavy cream
3 tablespoons maple syrup
Sea salt
Freshly ground black pepper

1 In a Dutch oven, melt the butter over medium-high heat, and add the onion, carrots, squash, and sweet potato. Cook for 15 minutes. Add the broth and bring to a boil. Reduce heat, cover, and simmer for 20 to 30 minutes, or until the vegetables are soft.

2 Remove the pot from the heat and cool slightly. Using an immersion blender (or in batches in a traditional blender), purée the

soup until smooth.

3 Reheat the soup over low heat. Swirl in the cream and maple syrup, and season with sea salt and pepper.

COOKING TIP: *If you prefer a chunkier texture, purée only half the soup.*

SWEET POTATO BISQUE

SERVES 6 TO 8 PREP TIME: 20 MINUTES COOK TIME: 40 MINUTES

With the addition of some croutons, grated Gruyère cheese, and a side salad, this delicious, nutritious soup would make the perfect vegetarian meal. Not only are sweet potatoes readily available, inexpensive, and highly versatile, they're packed with iron, potassium, magnesium, and vitamins B_6, C, and D!

GF V

2 tablespoons extra-virgin olive oil
3 or 4 onions, chopped
4 celery stalks, finely chopped
6 cloves garlic, finely chopped
5 sweet potatoes, peeled and diced
10 cups vegetable broth or stock
Salt
Freshly ground black pepper
2 cups half-and-half

1 Heat the olive oil in a Dutch oven over medium heat. Sauté the onions and celery for about 5 minutes, or until the onions are opaque. Add the garlic, and stir well.

2 When the garlic becomes fragrant, add the sweet potatoes and broth. Simmer, partially covered, for about 20 minutes, or until the

potatoes are tender.

3 Take the Dutch oven off of the heat and let the mixture cool slightly. Purée with an immersion blender (or in batches in a traditional blender) until smooth.

4 Season with salt and pepper, stir in the half-and-half, and reheat on low.

NUTRITION TIP: *For a spicy kick—one that will also aid digestion and help fight off colds—add ginger. Grate some peeled fresh ginger root (about 4 teaspoons) to add along with the broth or stock. Or use the same quantity of ginger paste, which can be found in the Asian section of most supermarkets.*

SHRIMP & CORN CHOWDER

SERVES 4 TO 6 PREP TIME: 10 MINUTES COOK TIME: 30 MINUTES

Impress your guests with this gourmet chowder that's incredibly simple and quick to prepare. Combining shrimp, potatoes, and corn in a creamy broth, it's a rich, satisfying bowl that's comforting and nutritious to boot.

GF **30**

2 tablespoons butter

½ **Vidalia onion, diced**

4 Yukon Gold potatoes (about 2 pounds), chopped

2 (16-ounce) bags frozen sweet corn, thawed

3 cups whole milk

1 cup half-and-half

1½ **pounds medium shrimp, peeled and deveined**

Salt

Freshly ground black pepper

1 In a Dutch oven over medium-high heat, melt the butter. Add the onion, and let sweat for 2 minutes.

2 Add the potatoes and continue to cook for 3 to 4 minutes, stirring frequently.

3 Add the corn, milk, and half-and-half, and simmer for 20 minutes, or until the potatoes are tender.

4 Add the shrimp to the pot, and stir. Cook until the shrimp turn pink, for 3 to 5 minutes.

5 Season with salt and pepper. Serve.

> **NUTRITION TIP:** *Shrimp is an excellent source of lean protein. Each 6-ounce portion provides 39 grams of protein at just 202 calories. It's also rich in vitamin, minerals, and amino acids—and mercifully low in mercury content.*

CREAMY BEET SOUP

SERVES 6 PREP TIME: 15 MINUTES COOK TIME: 40 MINUTES

Beets are synonymous with summer salads, but they can be so much more. This underrated root provides the base for this earthy autumn heart-warmer, thanks to its sweet taste and silky-smooth texture.

GF

2 tablespoons extra-virgin olive oil

2 cups chopped white onion

2 carrots, peeled and chopped

3½ cups peeled and diced beets

4 cups low-sodium chicken broth or stock

4 tablespoons heavy cream

2 teaspoons lemon juice

Sea salt

Freshly ground black pepper

1 tablespoon pesto, for garnish

1 In a Dutch oven, heat the olive oil over medium heat. Add the onion and carrots, and cook for 4 to 5 minutes, or until softened. Add the beets and cook for 6 minutes, or until the onion begins to brown.

2 Add the broth and bring to a gentle boil. Reduce heat to medium-low, and simmer for 20 minutes, or until the beets are tender.

3 Transfer to a blender or food processor, and blend until smooth, working in batches if necessary. Transfer the soup back to the Dutch oven, and return to medium heat.

4 Add the cream and lemon juice, and season with salt and pepper.

5 Divide the soup among serving bowls. Garnish each serving with a small dollop of pesto.

> **INGREDIENT TIP:** *Beets are available year-round, but winter is the prime time for baby beets, which are sweeter than mature ones. When buying, always choose small or medium beets, which are more tender than large beets. Check that they feel heavy for their size, have smooth, firm roots, and are free of nicks and cuts. If the greens are still attached, they should be brightly colored and have a fresh appearance.*

CHILLED CARROT SOUP

SERVES 4 TO 6 PREP TIME: 10 MINUTES COOK TIME: 30 MINUTES

Chilled soup makes a refreshing and light lunch on a hot summer's day. But the real beauty of this dish is that it goes with any season. Tweak the recipe by serving it piping hot during winter's deep freeze.

GF V 30

1 pound carrots, peeled and diced

½ cup extra-virgin olive oil, divided, plus more for garnish

1 shallot, finely diced

1 clove garlic, finely diced

1 tablespoon cider vinegar

Zest and juice of 1 orange

1 tablespoon grated fresh ginger

¼ cup cold water

Salt

Freshly ground black pepper

½ cup plain yogurt, for garnish

2 tablespoons coarsely chopped fresh tarragon, for garnish

1 In a Dutch oven over medium-high heat, bring salted water to a boil. Add the carrots and blanch until tender, about 5 minutes. Remove the carrots, set aside to cool, and empty the Dutch oven.

2 Return the Dutch oven to the stove, and heat 1 tablespoon of the olive oil over a medium-high heat. Add the shallot and sweat for 1

minute. Add the garlic and sweat for 1 minute. Remove the Dutch oven from the heat, and transfer the shallots and garlic to a small prep bowl. After the Dutch oven has cooled down, chill it in the refrigerator or freezer.

3 Place the shallots and garlic in a blender. Add the carrots, vinegar, orange zest and juice, and ginger, and pulse together until smooth. Add the cold water and blend until the soup has a smooth consistency. Reduce the speed to its lowest setting, and drizzle in the remaining 7 tablespoons of olive oil. Season with salt and pepper.

4 Return the soup to the chilled Dutch oven. Garnish with the yogurt, a drizzle of olive oil, and the tarragon.

> **NUTRITION TIP:** *Do carrots really help you see better in the dark? Yes! Carrots are rich in beta-carotene, which is converted into vitamin A in the liver. From there, the vitamin A is transformed into rhodopsin—a purple pigment necessary for night vision—in the retina.*

HEARTY BEEF STEW

SERVES 6 TO 8 PREP TIME: 20 MINUTES COOK TIME: 4 HOURS

This beef stew is a great make-ahead meal that tastes even better the next day. Make a double batch to freeze for those chilly autumn evenings that call for a warm, hearty pick-me-up.

GF DF

2½ pounds beef stew meat, cut into 1½-inch pieces
Salt
Freshly ground black pepper
2 tablespoons extra-virgin olive oil
3 onions, chopped
1 cup chopped celery
4 cups beef broth or stock
½ teaspoon dried thyme
½ teaspoon dried rosemary
3 to 4 potatoes (about 2 pounds, peeled and quartered
4 carrots, peeled and cut into 2-inch slices
2 cups frozen peas

1 Preheat the oven to 375°F.

2 Season the beef with salt and pepper. Heat the olive oil in a Dutch oven over medium-high heat. Add the beef and cook, stirring as

needed, until browned on all sides. Transfer the cooked beef to a plate.

3 Discard any excess oil from the pot, and return to medium-high heat. Add the onions and celery and cook until soft, or for about 3 minutes. Stir in the broth, thyme, and rosemary. Return the meat to the pot, and stir in the potatoes and carrots.

4 Cover, place in the heated oven, and bake for 3 hours.

5 Stir in the peas, and bake for 1 hour.

6 Season with salt and pepper.

INGREDIENT TIP: *For an extra antioxidant—not to mention an extra boost of flavor—add ¼ cup red wine right before adding the broth or stock. Bonus: The wine also helps preserve leftovers!*

BEEF & ROOT VEGETABLE STEW

SERVES 6 TO 8 PREP TIME: 40 MINUTES COOK TIME: 2 HOURS

This one-pot meal is the perfect antidote to dreary winter weather, adding an irresistible "welcome home" aroma to your kitchen. Feel free to substitute other vegetables, such as mushrooms or green beans, depending on what's in your pantry.

DF

3 tablespoons extra-virgin olive oil

3 pounds lean beef (chuck or round), cut into ½-inch cubes

5 leeks, chopped

¼ cup all-purpose flour

3 carrots, cut into 1-inch lengths

1 parsnip, peeled and chopped

1 white turnip, peeled and chopped

½ celery root (celeriac), peeled and cut into small cubes

1 bay leaf

2 large garlic cloves, thinly sliced

1 tablespoon roughly chopped fresh thyme leaves

2½ cups low-sodium beef broth or stock

Salt

Freshly ground black pepper

5 potatoes (about 2 pounds), peeled and quartered

1 (28-ounce) can crushed tomatoes

1 Preheat the oven to 350°F.

2 Heat the olive oil in a Dutch oven over medium-high heat. Begin adding the beef, a few pieces at a time. Brown on one side, then turn with a pair of tongs. Transfer the browned beef to a bowl, and repeat until all the beef is browned.

3 Pour off all but a tablespoon of fat in the pot, then add the leeks (see the tip below for how to clean leeks), and sauté over medium heat, stirring frequently, until they soften.

4 Toss the flour with the browned beef, then add the floured meat to the pot. Add the carrots, parsnip, turnip, celery root, bay leaf, garlic, thyme, and broth. Season with salt and pepper. Stir again and bring to a simmer on medium-high heat.

5 Cover, place in the preheated oven, and bake for 15 minutes.

6 Reduce the oven temperature to 300°F, and cook for 1½ hours.

7 uncover the pan and add the potatoes and tomatoes. Cover and cook for 25 minutes, or until the potatoes are tender. Remove the bay leaf before serving.

> **INGREDIENT TIP:** *To clean a leek, cut off the roots and slice the leek in half, lengthwise. Make crosswise cuts along the part of the leek that you intend to use—the last couple of inches of the dark green ends you can simply discard or save for broth or stock. Place the chopped leek in a bowl, and fill with cold water. Use your hands to agitate and dislodge any dirt clinging to the leek.*

FRENCH BEEF STEW

SERVES 6 TO 8 ■ PREP TIME: 1½ HOURS ■ COOK TIME: 2 HOURS

Roasted garlic gives an exquisite depth to this heart-warming stew, while Gallic flavors and red wine round out the robust symphony of aromas. You can make this ahead of time and reheat in the oven—after all, stews often taste even better the next day.

GF DF

1 head of garlic, papery skin removed and each clove cut in half
2 tablespoons extra-virgin olive oil, plus 2 teaspoons, divided
3 pounds chuck roast, trimmed and cut into 2-inch cubes
Salt
Freshly ground black pepper
1 cup red wine
2 tablespoons minced shallots
1 cup peeled and sliced carrots
1 cup peeled and sliced parsnips
5 ounces mushrooms, sliced
1 cup low-sodium beef broth or stock
1½ tablespoons tomato paste
Zest of half an orange
1 tablespoon herbes de Provence
1 bay leaf
1 (28-ounce) can diced tomatoes

1 Preheat the oven to 300°F.

2 Arrange the garlic in a Dutch oven, and drizzle with 2 tablespoons of olive oil. Cover and place in the pre-heated oven for about an hour, until the cloves start to pop out of their skins. Transfer the garlic to a small plate to cool.

3 Once slightly cooled, squeeze the cloves into a shallow bowl, and mash them with a heavy fork.

4 Place the Dutch oven on the stove top, and add the remaining 2 teaspoons of olive oil. Heat on medium-high until the oil is hot but not smoking. Add the beef cubes in batches, stirring them until evenly browned on all sides. Season each batch with salt and pepper, and then transfer to a small platter.

5 Add the wine to the pot and bring to a boil, scraping the bottom of the pot with a wooden spoon to loosen the browned bits. Stir in the meat, garlic, shallots, carrots, parsnips, mushrooms, broth, tomato paste, orange zest, herbes de Provence, bay leaf, and tomatoes. Bring to a boil, stir, and cover the pot. Place in the preheated oven.

6 Bake for about 2½ hours, or until the meat is tender. Remove the bay leaf before serving.

SPANISH LAMB STEW

SERVES 6 TO 8 ■ PREP TIME: 30 MINUTES ■ COOK TIME: 1½ TO 2 HOURS

Using inexpensive cuts of meat is a great way to make your budget stretch further. Thanks to the slow cooking of the Dutch oven, you don't have to compromise on flavor. Here, an otherwise tough cut of meat is simmered for almost two hours, which both tenderizes the meat and allows the rich Spanish flavors to permeate the lamb.

DF

2 tablespoons extra-virgin olive oil
2 pounds lamb stew meat, from the shoulder or leg, cut into 1-inch pieces
1 yellow onion, minced
Salt
Freshly ground black pepper
2 tablespoons all-purpose flour
3 cloves garlic, minced
1½ cups diced tomatoes (fresh or canned)
1 bay leaf
4 cups water
2 pounds fresh shell beans (cannellini beans, cranberry beans, black-eyed peas, or garbanzo beans), shelled
½ pound chorizo, sliced

1 In a Dutch oven, heat the olive oil over a medium-high heat. Add the lamb and onion, and season with salt and pepper. Cook, stirring occasionally, until the lamb is golden on all sides, for 8 to 10 minutes. Sprinkle the flour into the pot and stir. Cook for 2 minutes.

2 Add the garlic, tomatoes, bay leaf, and water. Bring to a boil over high heat. Reduce the heat to low, and simmer for 1 hour.

3 Add the beans and chorizo, and simmer for 40 minutes. Remove the bay leaf before serving.

COOKING TIP: *To take this stew to the next level, drizzle a spice-infused olive oil on top before serving. Warm 3 tablespoons of extra-virgin olive oil in a frying pan, and add 1½ teaspoons of paprika and 2 cloves of garlic, sliced. Pour the infused oil over the dish, stir gently, and let simmer for 30 seconds. Transfer the pot to the table and serve.*

CHICKEN & VEGETABLE STEW

SERVES 4 TO 6 ▪ PREP TIME: 20 MINUTES ▪ COOK TIME: 30 MINUTES

Bring a hearty taste to your midweek meal with this lowfat, one-pot wonder. Serve with rice or chunks of bread for a satisfying supper.

30

2 tablespoons extra-virgin olive oil
3 boneless chicken breasts
Salt
Freshly ground black pepper
Flour, for dusting
1 tablespoon unsalted butter
2 tablespoons all-purpose flour
1 yellow onion, chopped
2 celery stalks, chopped
4 cups chicken broth or stock
4 Roma tomatoes, chopped
1 teaspoon cumin
2 cups corn kernels (fresh, canned, or frozen)
2 cups frozen peas
½ cup thinly sliced scallions, for garnish
¼ cup roughly chopped fresh basil leaves, for garnish

1 Over medium-high heat in a Dutch oven, heat the olive oil until hot but not smoking.

2 Season the chicken with salt and pepper, and dust with flour. Brown the chicken in the olive oil. Using a slotted spoon, transfer the chicken to a plate.

3 Reduce the heat to medium-low, and add the butter and flour to the pot. Cook, stirring constantly, until the mixture is a rich brown color. (This will happen very quickly, so be diligent!) Stir in the onion and celery, and cook until both are softened.

4 Return the chicken to the pot. Add the broth, tomatoes, and cumin, and simmer, covered, for 15 to 20 minutes, or until the chicken is cooked through. Stir in the corn and peas.

5 Transfer the chicken to a chopping board. Using two forks, shred the chicken into bite-size pieces, and return to the stew.

6 Garnish with the scallions and basil before serving.

NUTRITION TIP: *To amp up the nutritional goodness of this healthy stew, replace frozen or canned vegetables with fresh veggies. About 4 ears of fresh corn off the cob will yield 2 cups.*

TUSCAN PORK STEW

SERVES 6 TO 8 ■ PREP TIME: 20 MINUTES ■ COOK TIME: 1 HOUR

This stew is inspired by ribollita, a hearty potage hailing from Tuscany. The word *ribollita* means "reboiled," which hints at its origins as a peasant dish made by reboiling the previous day's leftovers. Throughout the years, it's become a gentrified global palate pleaser.

GF **DF**

¾ **cup chopped bacon**
3 **tablespoons extra-virgin olive oil, divided**
2 **yellow onions, peeled and diced**
½ **pound hot Italian sausage, removed from casing**
7 **carrots, peeled and chopped**
¼ **teaspoon red pepper flakes**
Freshly ground black pepper
1 **tablespoon tomato paste**
7 **garlic cloves, peeled and chopped**
1 **(28-ounce) can diced tomatoes, undrained**
4 **cups chicken broth or stock**
1 **(16-ounce) can white cannellini beans, drained and rinsed**
Salt

1 In a Dutch oven over medium-low heat, cook the bacon in 1 tablespoon of olive oil for 5 to 6 minutes, stirring occasionally, until

most of the fat has been rendered and the bacon is beginning to crisp.

2 Add the onions and cook for 6 to 7 minutes, or until they become soft and translucent.

3 Add the sausage, carrots, and red pepper flakes. Season with black pepper and continue to cook for 10 minutes, breaking up the sausage into small pieces with the back of a wooden spoon.

4 Add the remaining 2 tablespoons of olive oil, stir in the tomato paste and garlic, and cook for 3 minutes. Stir in the diced tomatoes, broth, and beans. Season with salt.

5 Increase the heat to high until the soup starts to simmer. Reduce the heat to low, and simmer for 30 minutes.

> **COOKING TIP:** *In Italy, this stew is traditionally served with crostini—either added to the pot of soup about 5 minutes before serving (the classic way), placed in each bowl just before serving, or served on the side. Crostini are a cinch to make at home: Slice a baguette; season with salt, pepper, and a drizzle of olive oil; and toast.*

TURKEY, BEAN & CORN CHILI

SERVES 6 TO 8 ■ PREP TIME: 15 MINUTES ■ COOK TIME: 1 TO 1½ HOURS

A hot and hearty soup that's packed with protein and flavor. It's a great winter warmer for a crowd. This chili keeps well; serve up and reheat individual portions as needed.

GF **DF**

1 tablespoon vegetable oil
2 strips bacon, diced
1 onion, chopped
1 red bell pepper, diced
3 garlic cloves, chopped
1½ pounds ground turkey
¼ cup chili powder
2 teaspoons ground cumin
2 teaspoons dried oregano
Salt
Freshly ground black pepper
1 (15-ounce) can crushed tomatoes
1 ½ cups low-sodium chicken or vegetable broth or stock
1 (15-ounce) can pinto beans, drained and rinsed
1 (15-ounce) can sweet corn

1 Over medium heat in a Dutch oven, heat the vegetable oil. Add the bacon and cook until the fat is rendered and the bacon begins to

get crispy.

2 Add the onion and red pepper. Sauté, stirring often, until the vegetables are softened. Add the garlic and stir for about 2 minutes, or until the flavor is released.

3 Add the ground turkey and stir until no longer pink, gently breaking up the meat with the back of a spoon. Stir in the chili powder, cumin, and oregano. Season with salt and pepper. Stir in the tomatoes, followed by the broth. Bring the mixture to a boil, then reduce the heat to simmer.

4 Simmer, uncovered, for 45 minutes to 1 hour, stirring occasionally.

5 Carefully fold in the pinto beans and the corn, and simmer for 15 minutes.

> **COOKING TIP:** *You can make this dish look and taste unique each time you serve it by adding varying garnishments. Tasty topping options include extra-crispy bacon, chopped cilantro, shredded Cheddar cheese, sour cream, chopped scallions, diced olives, guacamole, and crushed tortilla chips.*

SMOKIN' BEEF CHILI

SERVES 8 TO 10 ■ PREP TIME: 20 MINUTES ■ COOK TIME: 1½ TO 2 HOURS

Combining two different meats, diced and ground, adds a really interesting texture to this chili. And slowly cooking the onions, peppers, and tomatoes into a jam like consistency makes for a beautiful depth of flavor—as does the addition of beer.

2 to 3 tablespoons extra-virgin olive oil
1½ pounds beef tri-tip or brisket, diced
1½ pounds ground beef
3 cups diced onions
4 garlic cloves, chopped
2 jalapeño peppers, diced
1 (8-ounce) jar roasted red peppers, drained and diced
½ cup tomato paste
1 tablespoon paprika
2 teaspoons cumin
2 teaspoons chili powder
1 (28-ounce) can crushed tomatoes
1 (12-ounce) can lager or stout beer
4 cups beef broth or stock
2 tablespoons brown sugar
1 (15-ounce) can kidney beans
Salt
Freshly ground black pepper
¼ cup sour cream or crème fraîche, for garnish
¼ cup sliced scallions, for garnish

¼ **cup shredded Cheddar cheese, for garnish**

1 In a Dutch oven over medium heat, heat the olive oil. Brown the diced beef and ground beef together in small batches, removing each batch to a large platter once browned. Drain excess fat from the pot, reserving 1 tablespoon.

2 Add the onions and garlic to the pot, and cook over medium-low heat until slightly translucent. Add the jalapeño peppers and red peppers, and continue to cook slowly until the mixture reaches a jamlike consistency.

3 Add the tomato paste and cook for 2 to 3 minutes. Add the paprika, cumin, and chili powder, and stir until fragrant.

4 Stir in the crushed tomatoes. Add the beer, broth, brown sugar, and beans, and season with salt and pepper. Return the browned meat to the pot, and bring to a boil, then reduce heat to a low simmer. Cook over low heat for 45 minutes to 1 hour.

5 Serve with a dollop of sour cream or crème fraîche, scallions, or shredded cheese.

> **COOKING TIP:** *To really amp up the texture of this chili, ask for freshly coarse-ground meat from your butcher. If you'd prefer the consistency to be a little thicker, add 1 or 2 tablespoons of flour.*

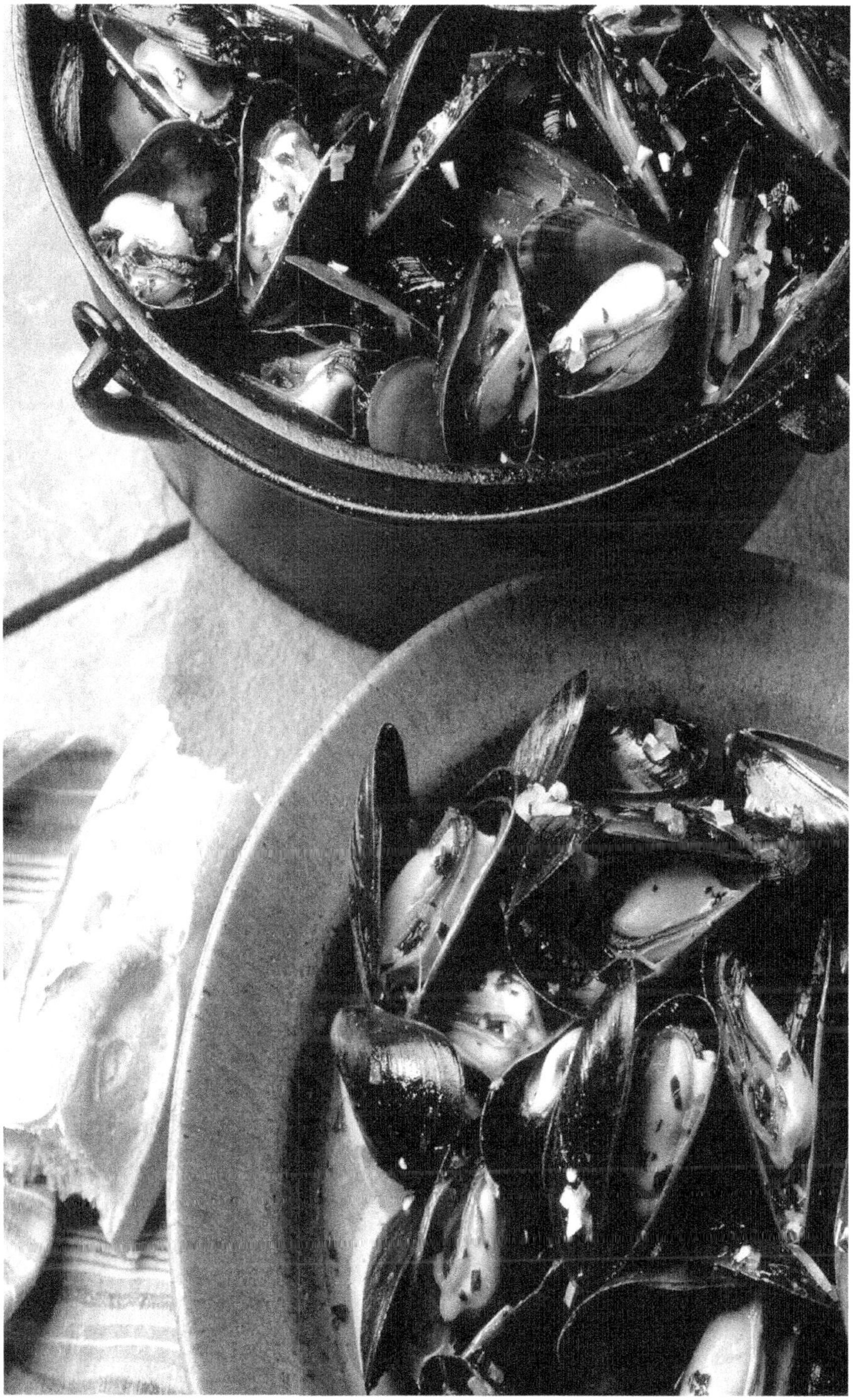

CHAPTER 4
FISH & SHELLFISH

SALT-CRUSTED CITRUS SNAPPER

SPICE-RUBBED SALMON

STEAMED MUSSELS WITH BACON

SPANISH PAELLA

LEMON-GRILLED HALIBUT

GRILLED SWORDFISH STEAKS

LINGUINE WITH CLAMS

SALMON WITH SPINACH

GROUPER WITH VEGETABLES

BOUILLABAISSE

SALT-CRUSTED CITRUS SNAPPER

SERVES 6 TO 8 PREP TIME: 15 MINUTES COOK TIME: 35 TO 40 MINUTES

Red snapper is a toothsome whitefish in season July through September, and available frozen all year. Because snapper fillets are so thin, roasting the fish whole ensures no meat goes to waste. If you prefer not to buy a whole fish, you can bake the fillets.

GF **DF**

2 pounds sea salt

¾ to 1 cup water

Cooking spray

1 large orange, sliced, divided

1 large lemon, sliced, divided

1 large grapefruit, sliced, divided

1 (4-pound) whole red snapper, cleaned and scaled

1 Preheat the oven to 375°F.

2 In a large bowl, combine the salt and water, and stir until it forms a pastelike consistency.

3 Coat a Dutch oven with cooking spray, then pour a 1-inch-thick layer of the salt mixture into the bottom of the pot. Layer half of the orange, lemon, and grapefruit slices on top of the salt. Place the red snapper on top of the slices. Press the remaining salt on top of the fish to form a thick crust. Top with the remaining fruit slices.

4 Cover, place in the heated oven, and bake for 35 to 40 minutes, or until the fish is done and the salt is lightly browned.

COOKING TIP: *Cooked fish should have an internal temperature of 145°F when checked in the center of the thickest part of the fish. To serve, crack the salt crust with the handle of a knife, flake the fish away with a serving fork, and top with the roasted citrus.*

SPICE-RUBBED SALMON

SERVES 4 TO 6 PREP TIME: 10 MINUTES COOK TIME: 20 MINUTES

To round out this delectable dish, serve on a bed of greens (butter lettuce is a mild option, or watercress lends a peppery kick). Drizzle the greens with lemon juice and olive oil, and season with salt and pepper.

GF DF 30

1 teaspoon kosher salt
1 teaspoon chili powder
1 teaspoon cumin
4 (6-ounce) salmon fillets, skin on
1 tablespoon extra-virgin olive oil

1 Preheat the oven to 375°F.

2 In a small bowl, combine the salt, chili powder, and cumin. Rub the salmon fillets with the spice mixture, coating them evenly.

3 Heat the olive oil in a Dutch oven over medium-high heat. Place the salmon fillets in the pot, skin-side up. Cook for 3 minutes, or until the tops are evenly browned. For medium-rare, flip and cook for 3 minutes. For medium to well-done, cover, place in the preheated oven, and bake for 5 to 10 minutes.

NUTRITION TIP: *In terms of health benefits, it's hard to beat the kingly salmon. This delicious, filling fish is rich in protein, omega-3 fatty acids, essential amino acids, and vitamins A, D, B, B_6, and E, as well as calcium, iron, zinc, magnesium, and phosphorus.*

STEAMED MUSSELS WITH BACON

SERVES 4 TO 6 PREP TIME: 10 MINUTES COOK TIME: 15 MINUTES

Mussels are not only quick to prepare, they're also inexpensive, readily available, and deliciously elegant. Mussels are sold and cooked live. Although they can live out of water for a few days, they should be kept well chilled.

GF **DF** **30**

2 to 3 tablespoons extra-virgin olive oil, plus more for garnish

½ cup bacon, diced

4 cloves garlic, thinly sliced

1 onion, chopped

1 cup dry white wine

2 teaspoons paprika

2 dozen mussels, cleaned and beards removed

Cayenne pepper, for garnish

Handful fresh oregano, chopped, for garnish

1 In a Dutch oven over medium heat, heat the olive oil and cook the bacon. Once the bacon fat begins to render, 2 minutes, add the garlic and onion. Cook, stirring, until they are translucent.

2 Add the wine and stir in the paprika.

3 Add the mussels. Increase the heat to high, and cook for about 30 seconds, or until the alcohol has evaporated.

4 Reduce the heat to medium-low. Cover the pot and steam for 5 to 8 minutes, until all the mussels have opened. Discard any mussels that haven't opened.

5 Garnish with a drizzle of olive oil, a sprinkle of cayenne pepper, and chopped oregano.

INGREDIENT TIP: *To clean mussels, place in a colander or bowl in the sink, and run them under cold water. Mussels attach themselves to surfaces using thin, sticky membranes called "beards." Most farm-raised mussels come debearded already, but if you find a bearded mussel, grasp it between your thumb and forefinger, and pull it firmly downward toward the hinged end of the shell until it comes out. Discard.*

SPANISH PAELLA

SERVES 6 TO 8 PREP TIME: 20 MINUTES COOK TIME: 45 MINUTES

Like so many other popular recipes, paella was originally a peasant dish made with whatever ingredients were available and cooked in a pot over an open fire—which makes it a perfect dish for a Dutch oven. This pared-down version of the iconic Spanish one-pot wonder is easy, quick, and a real delight.

GF DF

2 to 3 tablespoons extra-virgin olive oil
2 pounds chicken thighs, skinned, boned, and cut into 2-inch pieces
5½ cups low-sodium chicken broth or stock
½ pound shrimp, peeled and shells reserved
1½ pounds paella rice, or any Spanish-style medium-grain rice
¼ teaspoon saffron
1 (15-ounce) can cannellini beans, drained and rinsed
1 to 2 tomatoes (about ¾ pound), peeled, halved, seeded, and finely chopped
1 tablespoon smoked paprika
1 dozen mussels, scrubbed
Sea salt

1 In a Dutch oven over medium heat, heat the olive oil. Add the chicken pieces and sauté until golden. Using a slotted spoon,

transfer the chicken to a platter. Pour off the fat from the pot.

2 Return the pot to the heat, add the broth, and bring to a boil. Add the shrimp shells (reserving the shrimp), and simmer for 15 to 20 minutes. Remove the shells with a slotted spoon and discard. Stir in the rice and cook on medium heat for 10 minutes. Add the chicken pieces, saffron, cannellini beans, tomato, and paprika. Cook, covered, for 10 minutes.

3 Add the shrimp and mussels. Cook, covered, for 5 minutes, or until the mussels have opened.

4 Season with salt.

> **INGREDIENT TIP:** *There are two easy ways to peel tomatoes. One shortcut for removing the skin is to cut the tomato in half, seed it, and grate it on the large holes of a box grater. The other way—and by far the easier—is to dunk the tomato in boiling water and marvel as the skin easily slips off.*

LEMON-GRILLED HALIBUT

SERVES 4 TO 6 PREP TIME: 4½ HOURS COOK TIME: 15 MINUTES

Halibut is prized for its delicate sweetness, snow-white color, and firm, flaky flesh. An excellent source of high-quality protein and minerals, it's low in sodium, fat, and calories, and boasts a minimum of bones. This invigorating dish is a refreshing change from the hearty comfort foods of winter.

GF DF 30

6 halibut fillets

Juice and zest of 1 lemon

1 tablespoon roughly chopped fresh thyme leaves

1 tablespoon chopped fresh parsley

6 tablespoons extra-virgin olive oil, divided

Salt

Freshly ground black pepper

1 fennel bulb, sliced

½ teaspoon sea salt

1½ cups arugula

¼ cup fresh tarragon leaves

¼ cup chives, cut into ½-inch pieces

¼ cup fresh mint leaves

¼ cup fresh basil leaves

Salsa verde, for garnish

1 Season the halibut fillets with the lemon zest, thyme, and parsley. Cover and refrigerate for at least 4 hours.

2 Remove the fish from the refrigerator 15 minutes before cooking to bring it to room temperature. Brush with 2 tablespoons of olive oil, and season with salt and pepper.

3 Heat 1 tablespoon of olive oil in a Dutch oven over medium heat, and add the fish. Cook for 2 to 3 minutes, until it's nicely colored on the first side. Turn the fish over and cook a few minutes, until it's almost cooked through, and remove the pot from the heat (the fish will continue to cook).

4 In a large bowl, toss the sliced fennel with the sea salt, the remaining 3 tablespoons of olive oil, and 1 tablespoon of lemon juice. Add the arugula, tarragon, chives, mint, and basil, and toss, then season with salt and pepper. Arrange the salad on a large platter, place the fish on top, and garnish each fillet with a spoonful of salsa verde.

GRILLED SWORDFISH STEAKS

SERVES 4 ■ PREP TIME: 10 MINUTES ■ COOK TIME: 10 MINUTES

Firm fish steaks cook quickly on the stove top, and make a delicious and super healthy protein alternative. For an appetizing light lunch or supper, serve with avocado slices and your favorite salsa, and garnish with a wedge of lime. Feel free to substitute tuna steaks, if you prefer.

GF **DF** **30**

4 tablespoons extra-virgin olive oil, divided

2 teaspoons chili powder

2 teaspoons dried oregano, crumbled

1 teaspoon sea salt

½ teaspoon freshly ground black pepper

4 swordfish steaks, cut ¾-inch thick

1 Mix 3 tablespoons of olive oil with the chili powder, oregano, salt, and pepper. Brush the swordfish steaks with the oil mixture.

2 In a Dutch oven over medium heat, heat the remaining 1 tablespoon of olive oil. Add the swordfish steaks and cook for about 4 minutes. Turn and cook for a few minutes, until browned on both sides but still moist. It's best if the fish is slightly undercooked in the center, as it will continue to cook a bit after you've removed it from the heat.

INGREDIENT TIP: *When buying, look for "clipper" swordfish. This fish is frozen at sea, right after being caught, and is less expensive than "fresh, never frozen" varieties. Raw swordfish steaks should show a spiral pattern in the meat, with no dull or discolored skin. The meat will vary in color from a white or ivory to a pink or orange. Once cooked, it will have a beige tint.*

LINGUINE WITH CLAMS

SERVES 6 TO 8 PREP TIME: 20 MINUTES COOK TIME: 30 MINUTES

If you're looking for an easy meal guaranteed to impress, clams fit the bill perfectly. Cooks of all skill levels can prepare these tasty mollusks with confidence. It's impossible to give a specific amount of time required for cooking (it depends on size, quantity, and cookware used), so cook just until the shells pop open.

DF 30

2 (16-ounce) packages linguine
2 tablespoons extra-virgin olive oil, divided
4 cloves garlic, minced
3 (28-ounce) cans crushed plum tomatoes
4 teaspoons sugar
Salt
Freshly ground black pepper
2 pounds littleneck clams, cleaned
Fresh basil leaves, torn, for garnish

1 In a Dutch oven, cook the linguine according to the directions on the package. Drain and set aside.

2 In the same pot, heat 1 tablespoon of olive oil over medium heat. Add the garlic and cook for 1 minute. Stir in the tomatoes, the sugar, and the remaining olive oil. Reduce heat and simmer for 20 minutes, stirring frequently. Season with salt and pepper.

3 Add the clams. Cook for 5 minutes, or until the clams open. Discard any that don't. Stir in the linguine and toss to coat. Garnish with the basil.

> **INGREDIENT TIP:** *Clams should be washed thoroughly to remove any blemishes. Examine each shell and toss any that are cracked or damaged. Scrape off any barnacles with a knife. If there are any open shells in the batch, tap them with your fingernails or against a hard surface. If they don't close, throw them out—they're likely dead.*

SALMON WITH SPINACH

SERVES 6 ■ PREP TIME: 10 MINUTES ■ COOK TIME: 15 MINUTES

Salmon needs little in the way of embellishment. Just make sure not to overcook it—it should be just barely cooked in the center when the pot is removed from the oven. Wild-caught salmon is a cook's treasure, but farm-raised will do very nicely, too.

GF **30**

3 tablespoons unsalted butter

2 pounds fresh baby spinach

4 shallots, minced

6 salmon fillets

3 tablespoons fresh lemon juice

Sea salt

Freshly ground black pepper

2 teaspoons finely chopped fresh rosemary leaves

6 lemon wedges, for garnish

Horseradish cream sauce, for garnish

1 Preheat the oven to 325°F.

2 Coat the bottom of a Dutch oven, with the butter. Spread the spinach leaves evenly over the butter, and sprinkle with the minced shallots. Place the salmon fillets on the spinach, skin-side down, and drizzle with the lemon juice. Season with the salt, pepper, and rosemary.

3 Cover, place in the heated oven, and bake for 8 to 10 minutes. Uncover the pot and check the fish for doneness. If needed, finish the cooking with the pot uncovered for 3 to 5 minutes, or until the fish is opaque and the salmon flakes. Garnish with lemon wedges or a dollop of horseradish sauce.

GROUPER WITH VEGETABLES

SERVES 4 TO 6 PREP TIME: 20 MINUTES COOK TIME: 50 MINUTES

Grouper is a lean, firm, white-fleshed fish with a meaty texture and a flavor so mild and subtle, it appeals to even the pickiest palates. Though supply peaks in the warm months, from April to October, it's available all year round. This delicious one-pot dish is low in calories.

GF

2 pounds grouper
2 tablespoons extra-virgin olive oil
1 fennel bulb, thinly sliced
2 celery stalks, thinly sliced
6 shallots, skinned and chopped
Salt
Freshly ground black pepper
4 ounces butter, cut into small chunks
2 teaspoons chopped fresh dill

---

1 Remove the fine membrane covering the grouper. Remove the central bone (if the fish is not already deboned), and cut the fish into 1½-inch-thick diagonal slices.

2 In a Dutch oven over medium heat, heat the olive oil. Add the fennel, celery, and shallots, and cook until they begin to soften.

Transfer to a small bowl.

3 Brown the fish in the oil and transfer to a plate. Return the vegetables to the pot, then lay the fish on top. Season with salt and pepper.

4 Cover the Dutch oven and cook over a low heat for 5 minutes. Transfer the vegetables to a serving platter, and cover to keep warm. Cover the Dutch oven, and cook the fish for 30 to 40 minutes, or until tender.

5 Transfer the fish to the serving platter with the vegetables.

6 Place the Dutch oven back over the heat. Return the liquid to a boil, and stir in the butter. Add the dill and cook, stirring until thickened. Season with salt and pepper, and pour the butter sauce over the fish.

BOUILLABAISSE

SERVES 4 TO 6 PREP TIME: 30 MINUTES COOK TIME: 60 MINUTES

Bouillabaisse originated in the French seaport of Marseille, where the local fishermen made a stew from the bony rockfish they weren't able to sell to restaurants or markets. The recipe has been adapted over the years to include a seemingly endless array of ingredients, making it the ideal one-pot dish. Serve with thick cuts of country bread.

GF DF

3 tablespoons extra-virgin olive oil

6 garlic cloves, minced

1 to 2 onions (about ¾ pound), diced

1 shallot, minced

1 celery stalk, minced

1 carrot, diced

1½ tablespoons tomato paste

½ teaspoon saffron

1 teaspoon minced basil or 1 fresh basil leaf

2 tablespoons minced fresh parsley

Salt

Freshly ground black pepper 1 (28-ounce) can diced tomatoes, undrained

2 cups clam juice

1 (8-ounce) jar fresh oysters, juice reserved

1 pound whitefish (cod, halibut, or trout), cut into bite-size pieces

2½ pounds seafood mix (shrimp, clams, mussels, lobsters, scallops, crabmeat, or squid)

2 tablespoons chopped fresh parsley, for garnish

1 In a Dutch oven over medium heat, heat the olive oil. Add the garlic, onion, shallot, celery, and carrot, and sauté until lightly golden, about 20 minutes.

2 Add the tomato paste, saffron, basil, minced parsley, salt, and pepper. Mix well.

3 Add the tomatoes, clam juice, and juice from the jar of oysters. Bring the pot to a boil, lower the heat, and simmer for 15 minutes.

4 Add the oysters, whitefish, and seafood mix. Bring the pot back to a boil. Skim off any scum or fat. Lower the heat and simmer for 15 minutes.

5 Garnish with the chopped parsley.

COOKING TIP: *Cut your prep time in half by using a frozen seafood medley pack. You'll save a ton of time and the elbow grease otherwise spent on cleaning and cutting the seafood.*

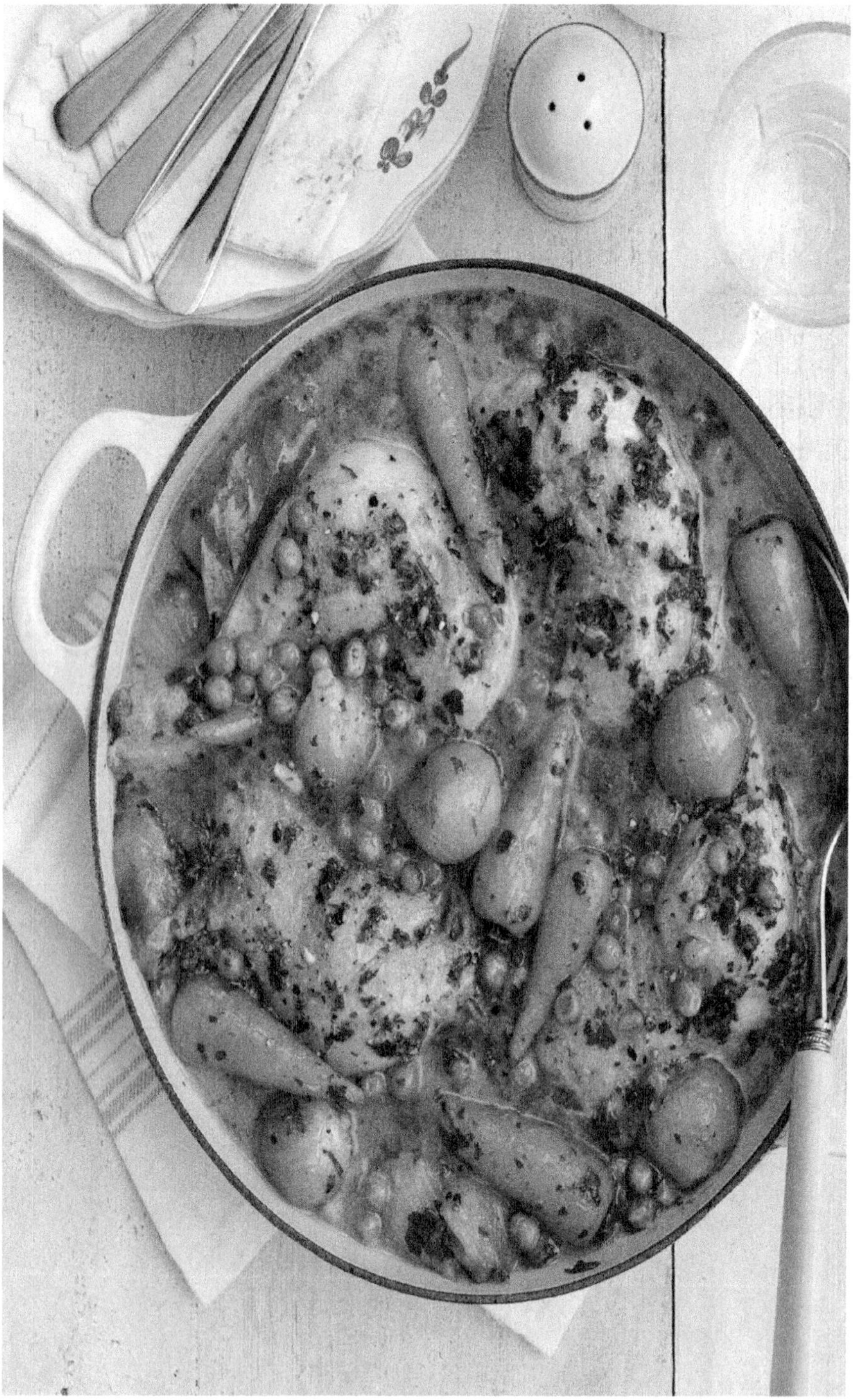

CHAPTER 5
POULTRY

CHICKEN CACCIATORE

HERBED CHICKEN WITH SPRING VEGETABLES

RICE WITH CHICKEN & CHORIZO

AROMATIC CHICKEN POT

CHICKEN & VEGETABLE STIR-FRY

CHICKEN WITH ONIONS & GARLIC

DUCK WITH OLIVE SAUCE

CHICKEN PASTA BAKE

LEMON ROAST CHICKEN

GOAT CHEESE-STUFFED CHICKEN BREASTS

CHICKEN, POTATO & BROCCOLI CASSEROLE

CHICKEN CACCIATORE

SERVES 4 TO 6   PREP TIME: 15 MINUTES   COOK TIME: 1 TO 1½ HOURS

Cacciatore means "hunter" in Italian. Allegedly, in the olden days, if a hunter were to return home empty-handed, his wife would go kill a chicken. This uncommon dish is centered on the common ingredients of chicken and vegetables.

GF **DF**

2 tablespoons extra-virgin olive oil

3½ to 4 pounds chicken thighs

1 onion, sliced

1 red bell pepper, seeded and sliced

8 ounces button mushrooms, sliced

2 garlic cloves, sliced

⅓ cup white wine

1 (28-ounce) can plum tomatoes

2 teaspoons chopped fresh thyme

2 teaspoons chopped fresh oregano

Salt

Freshly ground black pepper

---

1 In a Dutch oven over medium heat, heat the olive oil. Working in batches, cook the chicken pieces, skin-side down, until evenly browned, about 5 minutes. Turn over and repeat. Transfer to a platter and continue with the next batch.

2 Drain off all but 2 tablespoons of fat. Add the onion, pepper, and mushrooms to the pot. Increase the heat to medium-high. Cook about 10 minutes, stirring frequently, or until the onions are translucent. Add the garlic and cook for 1 minute. Add the wine and scrape up any browned bits at the bottom of the pot. Simmer until the wine is reduced by half.

3 Add the tomatoes. Stir in the thyme and oregano, and season with salt and pepper. Simmer, uncovered, for 5 minutes. Place the chicken pieces on top of the tomato sauce. Lower the heat and cover with the lid slightly ajar.

4 Cook on a low simmer, turning and basting from time to time, for 30 to 40 minutes, or until the chicken is tender.

HERBED CHICKEN WITH SPRING VEGETABLES

SERVES 6 PREP TIME: 10 MINUTES COOK TIME: 70 MINUTES

This recipe calls for garlic scapes, which are the tops of garlic plants harvested in the spring. Check at your local farmers' market for scapes in late May through late June. If you can't find garlic scapes, replace the scapes with four cloves of minced garlic.

2 tablespoons extra virgin olive oil

1 whole chicken, cut into individual pieces

Sea salt

Freshly cracked black pepper

1 onion, finely chopped

¼ cup finely chopped garlic scapes

3 tablespoons flour

1 cup dry white wine

2 cups chicken broth

10 baby carrots

2 cups pearl onions

2 cups peas

2 tablespoons chopped fresh thyme

¼ cup chopped fresh parsley

1 Preheat the oven to 350°F. Season the chicken pieces liberally with salt and pepper.

2 In a large Dutch oven, heat the olive oil over medium-high heat until it shimmers.

3 Working in batches without overcrowding the pot, brown the chicken pieces on all sides, about 5 minutes per side.

4 Set the chicken aside on a platter, tented with foil.

5 Add the onions to the oil in the pot and cook, stirring occasionally, until they are soft, about 5 minutes.

6 Add the garlic scapes and cook, stirring constantly, for 1 minute.

7 Add the flour to the pot and cook, stirring constantly, for 1 minute.

8 Add the white wine to the pot. Use a spoon to scrape any browned bits from the bottom of the pan.

9 Add the chicken stock, baby carrots, pearl onions, peas, and thyme to the pot.

10 Return the chicken to the pot, adding any juices that have collected on the platter. Stir together, and bring the mixture to a simmer.

11 Cover the Dutch oven, put it in the oven, and bake until the chicken is cooked through, about 40 minutes.

12 Remove the pot from the oven and stir in the chopped parsley. Serve immediately.

> **COOKING TIP:** *If you overcrowd the Dutch oven with the chicken pieces during the initial browning, the chicken will not brown effectively—it will steam. Therefore, it is best to work in two or three batches so the chicken has plenty of time to brown.*

RICE WITH CHICKEN & CHORIZO

SERVES 6 TO 8　PREP TIME: 15 MINUTES　COOK TIME: 1 TO 1½ HOURS

This venerable Mexican dish, called arroz con pollo south of the border, gets the down-home treatment in this Dutch oven recipe. Combining protein, grain, and vegetables in one lip-smacking burst of flavor, it's the perfect one-pot dish.

GF **DF**

8 skinless, boneless chicken thighs (or breasts, if you prefer)
Salt
Freshly ground black pepper
2½ tablespoons extra-virgin olive oil
1 onion, chopped
3 cloves garlic, minced
2 cups long-grain rice
2 teaspoons ground cumin
2 teaspoons crushed dried oregano leaves
5 cups low-sodium chicken broth or stock
1 green bell pepper, seeded and diced
1¾ cups thick and chunky salsa (mild, medium, or hot)
¾ pound spicy chorizo chicken sausage, diced
6 to 8 sprigs of cilantro leaves, for garnish
¼ cup chopped scallions, for garnish
6 to 8 lime wedges, for garnish

1 Preheat the oven to 350°F.

2 Trim any visible fat from the chicken, and season with salt and pepper.

3 In a Dutch oven over medium heat, heat the olive oil. Add half of the chicken pieces, and cook for about 3 minutes. Turn over and cook for 3 minutes, or until the chicken is lightly browned on both sides. Transfer the chicken to a platter, as they cook and repeat with the remaining pieces.

4 Add more oil to the pot, if needed, and add the onion. Cook until softened. Add the garlic and cook for 2 minutes, or until softened.

5 Add the rice, cumin, oregano, and some salt, and cook for 2 to 3 minutes, stirring until the rice is coated with oil. Stir in the broth. Add the green pepper and the salsa. Bring to a boil.

6 Cover, place in the preheated oven, and bake for 30 minutes, or until the liquid is almost completely absorbed.

7 Stir in the chorizo. Tuck the chicken pieces into the rice mixture, and pour in any juices that have collected on the platter. Cover, return to the oven, and bake for 20 minutes, or until the chicken is cooked through and the rice is tender.

8 Garnish with the cilantro leaves, chopped scallions, and lime wedges.

SUBSTITUTION TIP: *For a milder version of this feisty dish, substitute a can of sweet corn in place of the green pepper. For a spicier version, add a can of chopped mild green chiles.*

AROMATIC CHICKEN POT

SERVES 6 TO 8 PREP TIME: 15 MINUTES COOK TIME: 1½ HOURS

What could be better than a dish that practically cooks itself? The ingredients of this tasty chicken dish are quickly combined in the Dutch oven, then left to cook while you catch up on chores, take a hike, or finally start that book that's been languishing on your bedside table. Serve with rice for a filling and satisfying gluten-free meal.

GF DF

1 tablespoon vegetable oil
4 cups tomato sauce
3 garlic cloves, minced
1 large onion, chopped
2 bay leaves
2 teaspoons crumbled dried oregano
1 teaspoon ground chili powder
1 tablespoon red or white wine vinegar
Salt
Freshly ground black pepper
4 to 5 pounds chicken thighs (or a combination of thighs and legs), skinned but left on the bone

1 Preheat the oven to 350°F.

2 Combine in a Dutch oven the vegetable oil, tomato sauce, garlic, onion, bay leaves, oregano, chili powder, and vinegar. Season with salt and pepper, and stir to blend. Add the chicken to the pot, and stir to cover each piece with the sauce.

3 Cover, place in the heated oven, and bake for 1½ hours.

COOKING TIP: *This recipe is such a breeze, you'll return to it time and again. To mix things up, try adding chorizo sausage for a more exotic taste. For a spicier take on the dish, add a couple of 4-ounce cans of mild green chiles (drained). And for a more flavorful dish, add a sliced green or red bell pepper.*

CHICKEN & VEGETABLE STIR-FRY

SERVES 4 TO 6 PREP TIME: 15 MINUTES COOK TIME: 15 MINUTES

This dish is so delicious and surprisingly quick to prepare. Tender, flavor-packed chicken and lightly cooked vegetables make a healthy and hassle-free midweek meal. Marinating the chicken for even just a few minutes while preparing the vegetables makes all the difference.

DF 30

4 boneless, skinless chicken breasts, sliced
2 tablespoons soy sauce
2 tablespoons rice wine or dry sherry
2 garlic cloves, crushed
1 (1-inch) piece fresh ginger root, finely chopped
2 tablespoons peanut oil, divided
4 scallions, thinly sliced
4 ounces snow peas
4 ounces bok choy, chopped into bite-size pieces
1 (8-ounce) can bamboo shoots, drained
2 tablespoons hoisin sauce
Freshly ground black pepper

1 In a medium bowl, combine the chicken, soy sauce, rice wine, garlic, and ginger, and marinate while preparing the vegetables.

2 Heat 1 tablespoon of peanut oil in a Dutch oven over medium heat. Add the scallions and sauté for 1 minute. Remove the chicken from the marinade. Add to the pot and stir-fry briskly for 4 to 5 minutes, until cooked through and browned on all sides. Use a slotted spoon to remove the chicken from the pot.

3 Heat the remaining 1 tablespoon of peanut oil. Add the snow peas and bok choy. Stir-fry for 1 to 2 minutes. Add the bamboo shoots, and cook for 1 to 2 minutes.

4 Return the chicken to the pot. Add the hoisin sauce and stir. Season with a little black pepper.

COOKING TIP: *To cut your prep time in half, grab a package (12 ounces) of ready-sliced chicken strips. For a more robust meal, serve over rice and sprinkle with 2 teaspoons of sesame seeds.*

CHICKEN WITH ONIONS & GARLIC

SERVES 6   PREP TIME: 15 MINUTES   COOK TIME: 1½ HOURS

Onions, garlic, and saffron serve as an aromatic foil to chicken in this recipe that lets your Dutch oven do the heavy lifting, allowing you to supervise homework, hear all about your spouse's day, or catch up on your own! And do so safe in the knowledge that you'll be serving up a steaming hot pot of goodness.

GF **DF**

2 tablespoons extra-virgin olive oil
6 boneless, skinless chicken breasts
8 ounces pearl onions
2 garlic cloves, crushed
1 pound tomatoes, peeled and chopped
1 bay leaf
1 tablespoon roughly chopped fresh thyme leaves
2 tablespoons chopped fresh parsley
Pinch saffron
2 tablespoons dry white wine
Salt
Freshly ground black pepper
Juice of 1 lemon

1 In a Dutch oven over medium heat, heat the olive oil. Add the chicken and cook until each breast is a pale golden brown. Transfer

the chicken to a platter.

2 Add the onions and garlic to the pot. Cook over a low heat, stirring occasionally, until the onions begin to brown.

3 Stir in the chopped tomatoes, bay leaf, thyme, parsley, saffron, wine, salt, and pepper. Bring to a boil.

4 Return the chicken breasts to the Dutch oven. Cover and cook over low heat for 1 hour.

5 Stir in the lemon juice. Season with salt and pepper. Remove the bay leaf before serving.

DUCK WITH OLIVE SAUCE

SERVES 4 TO 6 PREP TIME: 15 MINUTES COOK TIME: 1 TO 1½ HOURS

Duck has a stronger, richer taste than other poultry. It's surprisingly unfussy to prepare, and provides a versatile base for many flavors. When buying, look for meat with a high-quality grading, such as USDA Grade A.

GF DF

1 tablespoon extra-virgin olive oil

6 duck breasts, skin scored

3 shallots, minced

2 garlic cloves

1 tablespoon roughly chopped fresh thyme leaves

1 bay leaf

1½ cups dry white wine

Freshly ground black pepper

½ cup pitted Kalamata olives

1 bouillon cube

1 cup water

1 Preheat the oven to 300°F.

2 In a Dutch oven over medium heat, heat the olive oil. Turn the heat to low, and sear half of the duck breasts, skin-side down, until crisp. Turn and lightly brown the other side. Using a slotted spoon,

transfer the duck breasts to a platter. Repeat for the remaining breasts.

3 Strain the fat from the pot. Add the shallots and garlic. Brown lightly, Add the thyme and the bay leaf, and sauté for 1 minute.

4 Add the wine, season with pepper, and reduce by half. Add the olives and sauté for 1 minute.

5 Return duck breasts to the pot, skin-side up. Add the bouillon cube and the water, and bring to a boil. Cover, place in the heated oven, and simmer for 30 to 45 minutes, or until the duck breasts are tender.

6 Remove duck breasts and place on a platter. Reduce the sauce, skimming the fat from the top. Ladle the sauce over the duck breasts and serve.

COOKING TIP: *Utilize the delectable duck fat by making a potato side dish. Reserve the fat after straining it from the pot. Once you've emptied the Dutch oven, add the duck fat, and heat over a medium-high heat. Fry a batch of peeled and sliced potatoes (about 1½ pounds) until golden brown. Season with a pinch of sea salt, and serve with the duck. Whatever you may decide for a side dish, be sure to save the strained duck fat for future recipes--it's a wonderful flavor booster, and can be stored in the freezer for up to a year.*

CHICKEN PASTA BAKE

SERVES 4 TO 6 PREP TIME: 10 MINUTES COOK TIME: 45 MINUTES

Casseroles are great for using up leftover ingredients in an interesting and delicious way. There is also something very satisfying about taking a hot casserole from the oven and placing it in the center of the table. Don't be afraid to substitute ingredients according to your preferences as well as what you've got in your refrigerator.

½ pound penne pasta

3 tablespoons extra-virgin olive oil, divided

1 onion, chopped

3 cloves garlic, minced

3 bunches kale, shredded

Salt

Freshly ground black pepper

1½ cups cooked shredded chicken

1 cup grated Gruyère cheese

Juice of 1 lemon

¼ cup grated Parmesan cheese

¼ cup panko crumbs

---

1 Preheat the oven to 375°F.

2 Bring a pot of salted water to a boil in a Dutch oven, and cook the pasta according to the directions on the package. Drain and set aside.

3 In a Dutch oven over medium heat, heat 2 tablespoons of olive oil. Cook the onion until translucent, or about 5 minutes. Add the garlic and sauté for 30 seconds. Add the kale to the pot, and season with salt and pepper. Stir a few times to wilt the greens. Cover, reduce heat to medium-low, and cook until the greens are tender, for about 10 minutes.

4 Add the pasta, chicken, Gruyère, and lemon juice to the greens, and season with salt and pepper.

5 In a small bowl, combine the Parmesan, panko crumbs, and the remaining 1 tablespoon olive oil. Sprinkle the mixture over the top of the pasta, and place in the heated oven, uncovered, for 30 minutes, or until the top is golden.

> **INGREDIENT TIP:** *Panko is a Japanese-style coarser type of bread crumb that is resistant to absorbing oil. You can substitute regular bread crumbs, but they won't have the same crunch.*

LEMON ROAST CHICKEN

SERVES 4 TO 6 ■ PREP TIME: 15 MINUTES ■ COOK TIME: 1 HOUR

You can't beat the wonderful aroma and the crackling sound of chicken as it roasts in the oven. This recipe proves that this classic dish doesn't have to be plain or boring. Add a few herbs and vegetables, and you'll have a one-pot roast that's bursting with freshness.

GF DF

4 lemons, cut in half, divided

1 medium (3½- to 4-pound) chicken, rinsed and patted dry, giblets removed

1 sprig rosemary

1 sprig thyme

1 sprig oregano

1 sprig parsley

Pinch salt

Pinch freshly ground black pepper

6 tablespoons extra-virgin olive oil, divided

1 tablespoon herbes de Provence

8 shallots, peeled

16 baby parsnips, peeled

1 Preheat the oven to 450°F.

2 Squeeze the juice from 2 lemon halves into the chicken cavity, and place the 2 halves inside. Add rosemary, thyme, oregano, parsley, salt, and pepper.

3 Loosely tie the legs together with kitchen twine. Rub 3 tablespoons olive oil over the chicken. Sprinkle with the herbes de Provence and another pinch of salt and pepper.

4 Coat the bottom of the Dutch oven with the remaining 3 tablespoons of olive oil. Place the chicken in the pot, and surround it with the shallots, parsnips, and the remaining 6 lemon halves.

5 Roast in the oven for 15 minutes. Lower the heat to 350°F, and roast for 45 minutes, or until the chicken juices run clear when the leg is pierced with a fork. Serve on a platter surrounded with the vegetables and lemons.

COOKING TIP: *Allow the roast chicken to stand for 15 to 20 minutes before carving, so the juices are reabsorbed into the meat.*

GOAT CHEESE–STUFFED CHICKEN BREASTS

SERVES 6 PREP TIME: 15 MINUTES COOK TIME: 30 MINUTES

This recipe is a surprisingly sophisticated take on chicken—and shockingly simple to make. Goat cheese–stuffed chicken breasts resting atop a bed of tender potatoes and asparagus pass all the criteria: fast, easy, affordable, and guaranteed to be a crowd favorite.

GF

FOR THE FILLING

4 tablespoons goat cheese

2 teaspoons chopped fresh thyme

Salt

Freshly ground black pepper

FOR THE CHICKEN

4 boneless, skinless chicken breasts

2 tablespoons extra-virgin olive oil, divided

12 ounces baby Yukon Gold or fingerling potatoes, halved

6 stalks asparagus, quartered

2 shallots, thinly sliced

Salt

Freshly ground black pepper

1 Preheat the oven to 375°F. In a small bowl, combine the goat cheese and thyme, and season with salt and pepper. Set aside.

2 Cut a deep pocket inside each chicken breast, using a sharp paring knife. Using your fingers, pack each pouch with a quarter of the goat cheese mixture. Gently press the opening closed. Season the chicken with salt and pepper.

3 In a Dutch oven over medium heat, heat 1 tablespoon of olive oil. Add 2 of the chicken breasts, and cook for 2 to 3 minutes per side, or until golden brown. Transfer to a platter. Repeat with the next batch.

4 Heat the remaining 1 tablespoon olive oil in the Dutch oven over a medium heat. Add the potatoes, asparagus, and shallots. Stir together, seasoning with salt and pepper.

5 Arrange the chicken breasts on top of the vegetables. Place in the oven, uncovered, and bake for 20 minutes, or until the potatoes are tender and the chicken is cooked through.

CHICKEN, POTATO & BROCCOLI CASSEROLE

SERVES 6 ■ PREP TIME: 10 MINUTES ■ COOK TIME: 2 HOURS

This rich, creamy casserole is sure to warm hearts and bellies alike on a cold winter's evening. Packed with protein and nutrient-rich veggies, it's both nourishing and nurturing—and a snap to prepare.

GF

Cooking spray

1 (15-ounce) can condensed cream of broccoli soup

1 cup sour cream

1½ cups shredded Swiss cheese

½ cup milk

6 cups cubed new potatoes

3 cups chopped cooked chicken

1 teaspoon Italian seasoning

Salt

Freshly ground black pepper

2 cups broccoli florets

¼ cup chopped fresh basil leaves

1 Preheat the oven to 350°F.

2 Lightly coat a Dutch oven with the cooking spray. Combine the soup and the sour cream. Stir in the cheese, milk, potatoes, chicken, and seasoning. Season with salt and pepper.

3 Cover, place in the heated oven, and bake for 1 to 1½ hours.

4 Stir in the broccoli. Return to the oven and bake, uncovered, for 10 minutes. Stir in the basil and serve.

STORAGE TIP: *Make a big batch and save leftovers: Divide into small, shallow containers for quick cooling in the refrigerator, and use within three to four days.*

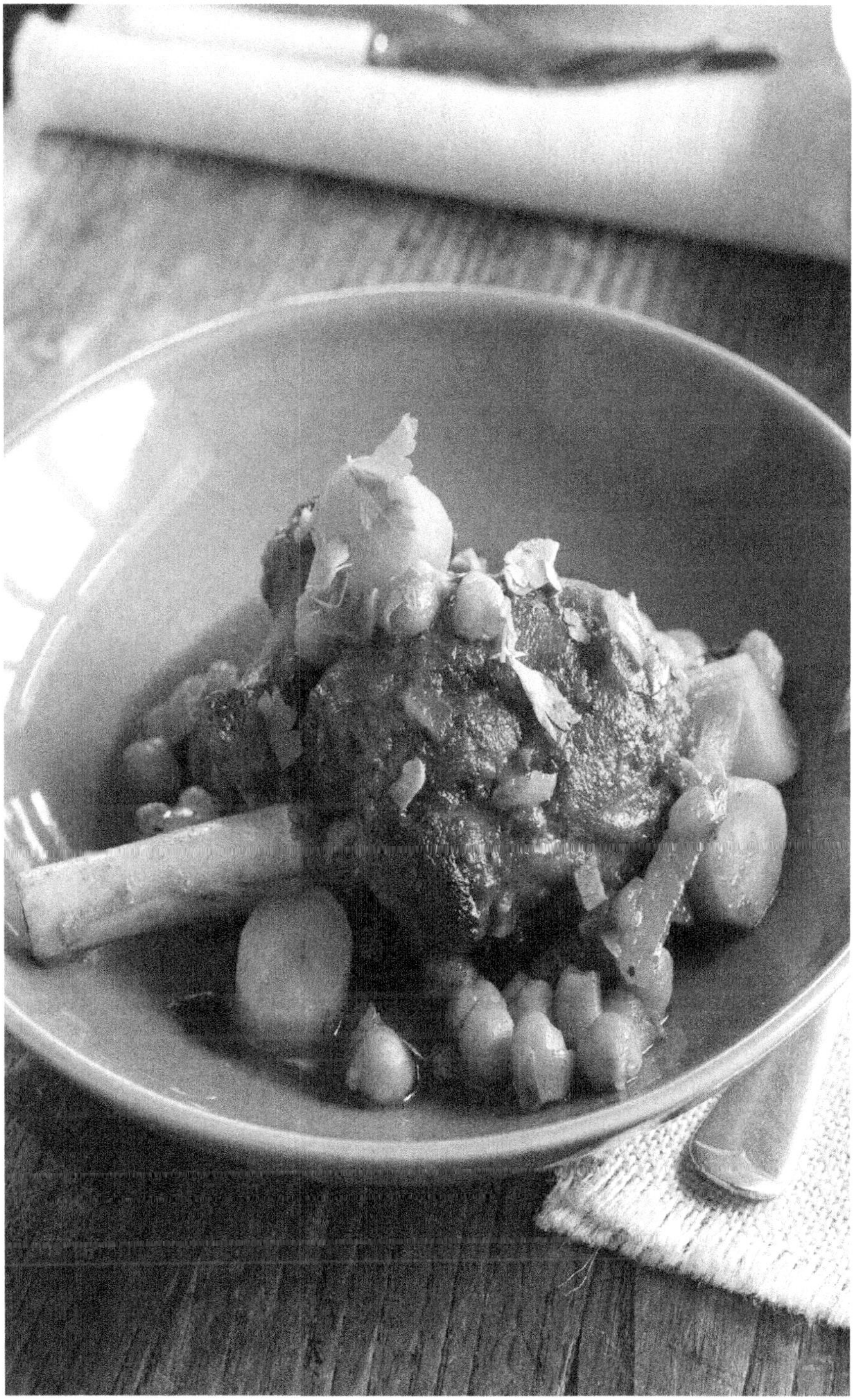

CHAPTER 6
PORK, BEEF & LAMB

CLASSIC PORK & BEANS

SPICY PORK WITH WINTER VEGETABLES

JERK PORK CHOPS WITH PLANTAINS

SHREDDED PORK BURRITOS

THREE-WAY PORK POT

PORK GOULASH

ROASTED PORK SHOULDER

PORK WITH RICE & BEANS

CAJUN RIBLETS

PORK RIB CASSEROLE

BEEF BOURGUIGNON

HERB-CRUSTED ROAST BEEF & POTATOES

- [BEEF TENDERLOIN](#)
- [BRAISED SHORT RIBS](#)
- [ROAST BEEF WITH ROOT VEGETABLES](#)
- [STUFFED MEATBALLS](#)
- [LAMB SHANKS WITH VEGETABLES](#)
- [SHEPHERD'S PIE](#)
- [LAMB CURRY](#)
- [BRAISED ROSEMARY LAMB SHANKS](#)

CLASSIC PORK & BEANS

SERVES 4 TO 6 PREP TIME: 10 MINUTES COOK TIME: 6 HOURS

The protein-packed pairing of pork and beans is ubiquitous in the American diet, and is most often associated with the chuckwagon days, when cattle-drive cooks used to rustle up beans, biscuits, and bacon for the voracious cowboys during the legendary three-month-long, six hundred-mile drives. This savory recipe recreates a piece of classic Americana—in the comfort of your own kitchen.

GF DF

1¼ pounds raw dried navy beans, soaked in water overnight
8 ounces salt pork, cut into ½-inch pieces
10 garlic cloves, peeled and cut in half
1½ cups minced onions
1 cup ketchup
¼ cup corn syrup
3 sprigs thyme
½ teaspoon dry mustard
Salt
Freshly ground black pepper

1 Preheat the oven to 300°F.

2 In a Dutch oven, cook the beans in boiling water for about 20 minutes, or until tender. Drain.

3 Add the pork, garlic, onions, ketchup, corn syrup, thyme, and dry mustard. Add water until the beans are covered, and season with salt and pepper. Cover, place in the preheated oven, and cook for 6 hours.

> **COOKING TIP:** *Don't worry if you're missing any of the preceding ingredients. A cookbook from 1832 (The American Frugal Housewife) lists only three ingredients for this dish: a quart of beans, a pound of salt pork, and pepper!*

SPICY PORK WITH WINTER VEGETABLES

SERVES 4 TO 6 ■ PREP TIME: 30 MINUTES ■ COOK TIME: 1½ TO 2 HOURS

Pork shoulder roast is an inexpensive cut that lends itself to braising and stewing. Spicy, sweet, and succulent, this slow-roasted one-pot recipe requires minimal prep work, and thanks to the Dutch oven, requires zero supervision during cooking.

GF **DF**

1½ pounds butternut squash, peeled, seeded, and cut into 1-inch pieces

1½ pounds sweet potatoes, peeled and cut into 1-inch pieces

1 tablespoon extra-virgin olive oil

¼ cup brown sugar

1 teaspoon ground cinnamon

1 teaspoon ground ginger

Salt

Freshly ground black pepper

2 onions, chopped

1 boneless pork shoulder roast (about 2½ pounds), trimmed of fat, cut into 1-inch pieces

1 cup low-sodium chicken broth or stock

1 Heat the oven to 300°F.

2 In a large bowl, combine the squash, sweet potatoes, and olive oil. Toss to coat. In a small bowl, combine the brown sugar, cinnamon, ginger, salt, and pepper. Sprinkle half of the sugar mixture over the squash mixture. Toss to coat. Transfer the squash mixture to the Dutch oven. Stir in the onions. In the same large bowl, combine the pork and the remaining sugar mixture. Toss to coat. Add to the Dutch oven, and then stir in the broth.

3 Cover, place in the heated oven, and cook for 1½ to 2 hours.

INGREDIENT TIP: *A tougher cut of meat, such as pork shoulder roast, is ideal for slow cooking. It contains more connective tissue, so it doesn't disintegrate when roasted slowly. And because it has more fat, it stays juicy and tender during cooking.*

JERK PORK CHOPS WITH PLANTAINS

SERVES 6 TO 8 PREP TIME: 1¼ HOURS COOK TIME: 35 MINUTES

Honey-glazed plantains make a sweet accompaniment to spicy jerk-style pork. If you don't have time to season the chops in advance, grill them as they are, adding a little seasoning to the pot to infuse the sauce with aromatic spice.

GF

8 pork chops
4 tablespoons extra-virgin olive oil, plus a splash for cooking
2 tablespoons onion powder
2 teaspoons thyme
1 teaspoon ground allspice
½ teaspoon ground cumin
2 teaspoons sea salt, divided
4 pounds ripe plantains, peeled and cut into 1-inch-thick slices
½ cup melted butter
½ cup honey

1 Rub the pork chops evenly with the 4 tablespoons of olive oil, onion powder, thyme, allspice, cumin, and 1 teaspoon of salt. Let stand for 1 hour.

2 Preheat the oven to 350°F.

3 In a Dutch oven over medium heat, heat the remaining splash of olive oil. Add half the pork chops, and cook for about 4 minutes. Turn over and cook for 4 minutes, or until the pork is lightly browned on both sides. Remove to a platter, and repeat with the remaining chops. Drain off all the fat. Cover to keep warm.

4 Combine the plantains, butter, honey, and the remaining 1 teaspoon salt in the Dutch oven. Cover, place in the heated oven, and bake for 20 minutes, or until tender and brown, turning once. Serve with the pork chops.

> **INGREDIENT TIP:** *Plantains have more starch and less sugar than bananas, often replacing potatoes and pasta in Caribbean recipes. Sold in the fresh produce section of the supermarket, they're available year round. Unlike bananas, plantains are cooked before serving, and function as veggies versus fruit.*

SHREDDED PORK BURRITOS

SERVES 6 TO 8 ■ PREP TIME: 10 MINUTES ■ COOK TIME: 4 TO 4½ HOURS

What could be easier than tossing all the ingredients in a Dutch oven and letting it take care of the cooking for you? Although this recipe calls for a long cooking time, supervision of the cooking requires minimal effort. Braising the pork slowly in the oven yields meat that's tender, tasty, and rich with flavor.

GF **DF**

FOR THE PORK
1 large onion, chopped
4 cloves garlic, crushed
1 bone-in pork shoulder (4 to 5 pounds)
1 tablespoon coriander seeds
1 tablespoon cumin seeds
2 teaspoons dried oregano leaves
3 canned chipotle chiles
2 bay leaves
Salt

FOR SERVING
Corn tortillas, warmed
Salsa, for garnish
Lime wedges, for garnish
Sliced avocados, for garnish
Chopped cilantro, for garnish

1 Preheat the oven to 450°F.

2 In a Dutch oven, place the onion, garlic, pork, coriander, cumin, oregano, chipotle chiles, and bay leaves. Add enough water to cover the meat. Place over a medium-high heat, cover, and bring to a boil. Reduce the heat and simmer until the meat falls away from the bone (3 to 4 hours).

3 Remove the meat to a platter. Pour the broth into a container and set aside.

4 Return the meat to the Dutch oven, and place it in the heated oven, uncovered. Bake until the pork is browned, and discard the bay leaves.

5 Shred the pork coarsely with two forks, discarding any fat. Season with salt. Heap the meat mixture into the tortillas, and garnish with the salsa, lime wedges, avocados, or cilantro.

STORAGE TIP: *The pork broth is so delicious, we recommend you reserve it and use it later in soups and stews. After pouring it off, use a spoon to remove any surface fat, and refrigerate or freeze.*

THREE-WAY PORK POT

SERVES 6 TO 8 ▪ PREP TIME: 30 MINUTES ▪ COOK TIME: 3½ TO 4 HOURS

This recipe is a meat lover's dream. Three cuts of pork are cooked slowly in an aromatic broth to release the flavor gradually and tenderize the meat so that it melts in your mouth. All that goodness, plus a healthy serving of veggies, makes for a sensational and satisfying one-pot meal.

GF **DF**

1½ pounds pork belly, fat trimmed, and scored in diamond pattern
1 rack pork ribs
2 pork shanks
5 garlic cloves, chopped
4 shallots, diced
2 thyme sprigs
½ cup dark brown sugar
2 bay leaves
Freshly ground black pepper
1 quart chicken broth or stock
12 ounces white, navy, or cannellini beans
1 (15-ounce) can diced tomatoes
1 cup dry white wine
6 ounces baby carrots
2 celery stalks, cut into 2-inch pieces
6 ounces pearl onions
1 tablespoon cornstarch

1 Preheat the oven to 275°F.

2 Place the pork belly, ribs, and shanks in a Dutch oven, and cover with water. Bring to a boil, then drain and rinse the pork.

3 Return the pork to the pot. Add the garlic, shallots, thyme, dark brown sugar, and bay leaves. Season with pepper. Bring to a boil. Cover, place in the preheated oven, and cook for 2 hours.

4 Transfer the pork to a platter. Strain and save the broth, discarding the thyme and bay leaves.

5 use two forks to pull the meat off the shanks, and dice the pork belly into 2-inch pieces.

6 Place the pork and the broth back into the pot. Add the beans, tomatoes, and wine. Cover and simmer over low heat for about 1 hour, or until the beans are almost tender.

7 Add the carrots, celery, and pearl onions. Cover and cook for about 15 minutes, until tender.

8 Transfer the meat and vegetables to a serving platter. Bring the remaining liquid to a boil, and thicken with a mixture of cornstarch and 1 tablespoon water. Ladle the sauce over the meat and vegetables. Serve.

> **INGREDIENT TIP:** *When shopping for pork, there are a few tricks to selecting the best quality money can buy. Always make sure the pork meat has a pinkish-red color, and avoid any cuts that are pale-hued. Choose meat that has marbling or small flecks of fat—the more marbling, the more savor. Just check that the fat is white, with no dark spots. Also, avoid choosing any meat with dark-colored bones.*

PORK GOULASH

SERVES 4 TO 6 PREP TIME: 15 MINUTES COOK TIME: 3 HOURS

Goulash is the national dish of Hungary. A stew of meat and vegetables, seasoned with paprika and other spices, this is a great make-ahead dish. Let the goulash cool to room temperature, and refrigerate, pot and all. When ready to serve, bring the pot back up to room temperature. Reheat in a 325°F oven for about 30 minutes, or until the goulash is warmed through.

GF

5 slices bacon, diced
2 sweet onions, roughly chopped
1½ tablespoons Hungarian paprika
2 pounds boneless lean pork, cut into 1-inch cubes
Salt
Freshly ground black pepper
1 (15 ounce) can diced tomatoes
1 teaspoon dried marjoram, crumbled
2 garlic cloves, finely chopped
1½ cups dry white wine
1 cup chicken broth or stock
Low-fat sour cream, for garnish
Finely chopped fresh parsley, for garnish

1 Preheat the oven to 425°F.

2 In a Dutch oven, put the bacon pieces. Cover, place in the preheated oven, and cook for about 20 minutes, or until the fat is rendered. Reduce the temperature to 350°F. Add the onions. Stir, cover, and let the onions cook for about 30 minutes, or until translucent and golden. Stir in the paprika.

3 Season the pork cubes with the salt and pepper. Add to the pot and stir. Cover, return to the oven, and cook for 20 minutes.

4 Add the tomatoes, marjoram, and garlic. Stir in the wine and the broth.

5 Cover, return to the oven, and cook for 1½ to 2 hours, stirring occasionally, until the meat is tender.

6 Serve garnished with sour cream and parsley.

> **INGREDIENT TIP:** *Use Hungarian paprika for this dish, you'll find it in the supermarket. Paprika is the national spice of Hungary, and because goulash is the national dish, is used prominently in any goulash recipe you'll find.*

ROASTED PORK SHOULDER

SERVES 6 ■ PREP TIME: 10 MINUTES ■ COOK TIME: 9½ TO 10½ HOURS

Slow cooked for around 10 hours, the meat melts off the bone. Although the cooking time is long, it requires minimal supervision, thanks to the Dutch oven's ability to cook slowly and uniformly. Prep this dish in the morning, and treat your family to a mouthwatering feast in the evening. Serve with braised greens or mashed potatoes.

GF **DF**

4 parsnips, roughly chopped
4 carrots, roughly chopped
3 onions, roughly chopped
3 garlic bulbs, cloves roughly smashed
1 bunch fresh thyme, chopped
1 pork shoulder (5-6 pounds)
3 tablespoons extra-virgin olive oil
1 cup balsamic vinegar
1 cup white wine
2 cups chicken broth or stock

1 Preheat the oven to 450°F.

2 In a Dutch oven, combine the parsnips, carrots, onions, garlic, and thyme. Rub the pork shoulder with the olive oil, and place it on top of the vegetables. Add the vinegar, wine, and broth.

3 Place the pot, uncovered, in the preheated oven, and cook for 30 minutes. Lower the temperature to 250°F, cover, and cook for 9 to 10 hours, or until the meat is soft and can be pulled apart easily with a fork.

> **COOKING TIP:** *Once the pork is out of the oven, let it stand for 30 minutes before serving. By letting it rest, the juices will be reabsorbed back into the meat, and the pork will be perfectly tender and juicy upon tasting.*

PORK WITH RICE & BEANS

SERVES 6 PREP TIME: 10 MINUTES COOK TIME: 2½ TO 3 HOURS

The most overlooked cuts of meat oftentimes are the most toothsome. A ham hock is a thick cut of pork that comes from a pig's leg, between the ham and the foot. It's inexpensive and tasty on its own, and adds a ton of flavor to a pot of soup, stew, or beans.

GF DF

1 (15-ounce) can red kidney beans
1 smoked pork hock (about 1½ pounds)
12 ounces chorizo, cut into ½-inch pieces
2½ cups low-sodium chicken broth or stock
1 onion, chopped
1 stalk celery, chopped
1 tablespoon tomato paste
2 cloves garlic, minced
½ teaspoon crushed dried thyme
½ teaspoon crushed dried oregano
3½ cups precooked long-grain rice

1 Preheat the oven to 300°F.

2 In a Dutch oven, combine the beans, pork hock, chorizo, broth, onion, celery, tomato paste, garlic, thyme, and oregano. Cover, place in the heated oven, and cook for 2 to 2½ hours.

3 Remove the pork hock from the pot. Slice the meat off the bone, and cut it into bite-size pieces. Stir the meat back into the bean mixture, add the rice, and return to the oven. Cook for 10 to 15 minutes, or until the rice is heated through.

> **STORAGE TIP:** *Leftovers? Save them for tomorrow. Pork should be placed in the refrigerator within one to two hours of serving. Cooked pork stored in the coldest part of the refrigerator will stay fresh for four to five days. Well-wrapped leftovers can be kept in the freezer for up to three months.*

CAJUN RIBLETS

SERVES 6 PREP TIME: 20 MINUTES COOK TIME: 1 TO 1½ HOURS

This recipe uses loin back ribs (also known as baby back ribs), a tender cut of pork found just under the back fat of the pig. Usually reserved for backyard barbecues, this dish proves you don't need a grill to make ribs—and they'll still be finger-licking good!

GF **DF**

2 pounds pork loin back ribs
1 tablespoon Cajun seasoning
1 cup chili sauce
1 onion, chopped
1 tablespoon cornstarch
1 jalapeño pepper, seeded and finely chopped
1 tablespoon lemon juice
1 to 2 teaspoons hot pepper sauce

1 Preheat the oven to 300°F.

2 Sprinkle the pork ribs with the Cajun seasoning. Cut them into single-rib portions, and place in the Dutch oven.

3 In a medium bowl, combine the chili sauce, onion, cornstarch, jalapeño pepper, lemon juice, and hot pepper sauce. Pour the mixture over the ribs.

4 Cover, place in the preheated oven, and cook for 1 to 1½ hours.

> **INGREDIENT TIP:** *Jalapeño, like all chile peppers, contains oils that can burn your skin and eyes, so avoid direct contact with them when cooking. Wear plastic or rubber gloves or, if not possible, wash your hands well with soap and warm water immediately after handling.*

PORK RIB CASSEROLE

SERVES 4 TO 6 PREP TIME: 10 MINUTES COOK TIME: 2 TO 2½ HOURS

When it comes to winter comfort food, it's hard to beat the taste of a slow-cooked casserole. And a casserole is so easy to make. In this one, pork ribs, pinto beans, and peppers are combined in the Dutch oven, seasoned with chili powder and cumin, and left to cook to perfection as the flavors are slowly released.

GF DF

1 tablespoon vegetable oil
2 pounds boneless pork country-style ribs
1 red bell pepper, seeded and chopped
1 poblano chile, seeded and chopped
1½ teaspoons bottled minced garlic
2 (15-ounce) cans pinto beans, rinsed and drained
1 (28-ounce) can crushed tomatoes
1 medium onion, chopped
1 tablespoon chili powder
1 teaspoon ground cumin
Salt
Freshly ground black pepper

1 Preheat the oven to 325°F.

2 Heat the vegetable oil in a Dutch oven over a medium heat. Cook the pork ribs, in batches, until browned on both sides. Transfer the ribs to a plate, and drain off the fat from the pot.

3 In the Dutch oven, combine the bell and poblano peppers, garlic, beans, tomatoes, onion, chili powder, cumin, salt, and pepper. Add the ribs.

4 Cover, place in the oven, and cook for 2 to 2½ hours, or until the meat is tender.

5 On a clean work surface, break the ribs apart into serving-size pieces. Return to the pot, stirring to combine. Serve in the Dutch oven with a side of cornbread.

> **INGREDIENT TIP:** *The poblano is one of the most popular chile peppers in Mexican cuisine. Large and luscious, with a beautiful dark-green color that looks almost black, it can enhance roasts, stews, casseroles, chilies, and sauces—just don't eat it raw.*

BEEF BOURGUIGNON

SERVES 6 TO 8 PREP TIME: 30 MINUTES COOK TIME: 3 TO 3½ HOURS

This traditional French dish hails from the Burgundy region. Our recipe stays true to the classic combination of beef braised in red wine (typically, a Burgundy) and beef broth or stock, and flavored with garlic and onions. Despite its origins as a peasant dish, beef bourguignon is a sophisticated stew that will impress any crowd.

GF

2½ pounds chuck beef, cut into 1-inch cubes
Salt
Freshly ground black pepper
¾ cup gluten-free flour (made from fava beans or garbanzo beans), divided
4 tablespoons extra-virgin olive oil
6 ounces applewood-smoked bacon, diced
12 pearl onions, peeled
12 baby carrots, peeled and halved
1 pound mushrooms, sliced
2 tablespoons butter
2 onions, diced
6 cloves garlic, peeled and chopped
2 tablespoons tomato paste
½ teaspoon dried thyme
1 (750-milliliter) bottle dry red Burgundy wine
1 quart beef broth or stock

1 Preheat the oven to 325°F.

2 Season the beef cubes with salt and pepper, then lightly coat with ½ cup of flour.

3 In a Dutch oven over medium heat, heat the olive oil. Cook the bacon until the fat is rendered. Transfer to a platter. Working in batches, sear the beef in the hot fat for 3 to 5 minutes, until brown on all sides. Transfer to the platter with the bacon, and continue searing until all the beef is browned.

4 Add the pearl onions, carrots, and mushrooms to the pot, and cook for 2 to 3 minutes. Transfer to a platter.

5 Add the butter to the pot. Add the onions and garlic, and cook for 4 to 5 minutes, or until transparent.

6 Stir in the remaining ¼ cup flour, the tomato paste, and the thyme. Cook for 2 minutes.

7 Doglaze the pot with the wine, and bring to a boil. Pour in the broth, and again return to a boil.

8 Return the bacon and beef cubes to the pot. Bring to a boil. Cover, place in the heated oven, and cook for 2 to 2½ hours.

9 Return the pearl onions, carrots, and mushrooms to the pot. Cook for 30 minutes.

INGREDIENT TIP: *The chuck section of beef comes from the shoulder and neck of the animal. This delectable cut of meat is easy on the wallet. The fact that it's on the tough and fatty side makes it perfect for slow cooking, because the meat stays tender without breaking up in the oven.*

HERB-CRUSTED ROAST BEEF & POTATOES

SERVES 6 PREP TIME: 10 MINUTES COOK TIME: 1 TO 1½ HOURS

Eye of round is a fairly inexpensive and extremely lean cut taken from the hindquarters of the cow. The larger the roast, the longer it will take to cook—and the more tasty the leftovers you'll have for sandwiches. Precooking the potatoes ensures they'll be done when the roast is cooked to your liking.

GF DF

12 baby new potatoes (about 1½ pounds)
1 teaspoon sea salt
1 teaspoon black pepper
4 garlic cloves, minced
1 teaspoon dried thyme
1 teaspoon dried rosemary
2 tablespoons Dijon mustard
3 pounds eye of round roast

---

1 Preheat the oven to 325°F.

2 In a Dutch oven on medium heat, bring water to a boil. Boil the potatoes until they are just barely cooked through. Transfer to a bowl.

3 Mix the salt, pepper, garlic, thyme, rosemary, and mustard into a paste, and spread it over the roast. Place the meat in the Dutch

oven, fatty-side up, and roast for about 20 minutes per pound, or until the internal temperature registers 125°F for rare, 150°F for medium, or 160°F for well-done.

4 About 30 minutes before the beef is cooked to your liking, add the potatoes to the pot, turning them on all sides.

BEEF TENDERLOIN

SERVES 6 PREP TIME: 15 MINUTES COOK TIME: 1½ HOURS

This special occasion dish utilizes the most tender cut of beef—the tenderloin. Cut from the spine area, beneath the ribs and next to the backbone—near the butt of the cow—it's a part of the muscle structure that doesn't do very much work and therefore yields the softest meat. Opt for this recipe when you want to pull out all the stops.

¾ pound shallots, peeled and halved lengthwise
2 tablespoons extra-virgin olive oil, divided
Salt
Freshly ground black pepper
3 cups beef broth or stock
1½ teaspoons tomato paste
3 slices bacon, diced
1 (2-pound) beef tenderloin
1 teaspoon dried thyme
2 tablespoons softened butter
1 tablespoon all-purpose flour

1 Preheat the oven to 350°F.

2 In a Dutch oven, combine the shallots and 1 tablespoon of olive oil. Season with salt and pepper. Bake in the heated oven for about 30 minutes, or until the shallots are browned. Transfer to a platter.

3 Bring the broth to a boil in the Dutch oven over high heat. Stir in the tomato paste, and transfer the mixture to a bowl.

4 Heat the remaining 1 tablespoon olive oil in the pot over medium heat, and cook the bacon for 7 to 10 minutes, or until the bacon is browned and crispy. Transfer to the platter with the shallots.

5 Season the tenderloin with the thyme, salt, and pepper. Add to the pot and cook over medium heat until browned on all sides, about 7 minutes. Cover, place in the oven, and bake until medium-rare, or an internal thermometer registers 130-135°F, about 25 minutes.

6 Transfer the tenderloin to a platter. Skim away any excess fat from the pot, and place the pot back on the stove top. Return the broth mixture to the pot and bring to a boil, scraping the bottom and sides of the pot with a wooden spoon to loosen any browned bits. Reduce the heat to low. Whisk in the butter and flour, and cook for 2 to 3 minutes, or until the sauce thickens. Return the shallots and bacon to the pot. Season with salt and pepper.

7 Cut the tenderloin into ½-inch-thick slices. Arrange on a serving dish and spoon the sauce on top.

COOKING TIP: *A few sprigs of watercress is a lovely garnish for this rich dish. Add potatoes and roasted asparagus as side dishes to round out the culinary feast.*

BRAISED SHORT RIBS

SERVES 6 TO 8 PREP TIME: 10 MINUTES COOK TIME: 4 TO 4½ HOURS

One of the best cuts of meat for long, slow cooking, beef short ribs—if cooked properly—are fall-off-the-bone tender, and a definite crowd-pleaser. If you'd like a starchy side for the meat, go Italian style and dish up egg noodles or creamy polenta.

DF

8 beef short ribs
Salt
Freshly ground black pepper
All-purpose flour, for dredging
¼ cup plus 2 tablespoons vegetable oil, divided
1 onion, diced
2 large carrots, peeled and diced
1½ cups red wine
1 large (28-ounce) can crushed tomatoes
1 bay leaf

1 Preheat the oven to 300°F.

2 Season the short ribs with salt and pepper, then lightly coat them with the flour.

3 In a Dutch oven over medium heat, heat ¼ cup of vegetable oil, and cook the ribs on all sides until evenly browned. Transfer the ribs

to a platter.

4 Reduce the heat to medium-low, and add the remaining 2 tablespoons vegetable oil, the onion, and the carrots to the pot. Cook for 15 to 20 minutes, until the vegetables are evenly browned.

5 Return the short ribs to the pot and add the wine. Raise the heat to medium-high. Add the tomatoes, a pinch of salt, and the bay leaf, and bring the mixture to a simmer.

6 Cover, place in the heated oven, and bake for 3 to 4 hours, or until the ribs are very tender. Remove the pot from the oven and let cool slightly.

7 Skim off any clear fat that has risen to the top of the sauce, and discard. Spoon the defatted sauce over the ribs, and serve.

COOKING TIP: If you want to get extra-fancy, garnish each plate with gremolata, an easy-to-make and tasty chopped-herb condiment made with lemon zest, minced garlic, and chopped parsley. Just mix together 1 tablespoon each of lemon zest and garlic with 2 tablespoons of parsley. If you don't have parsley on hand, cilantro, mint, or sage will substitute nicely.

ROAST BEEF WITH ROOT VEGETABLES

SERVES 6 TO 8 ■ PREP TIME: 20 MINUTES ■ COOK TIME: ABOUT 1½ HOURS

Prime rib is considered the king of beef cuts. Beautifully marbled with fat, this roast is rich, juicy, and tender. It's also very easy to cook. Served with roasted root vegetables, it makes the perfect holiday or special occasion dish. Don't be afraid to make extra—it tastes just as good the next day, sliced cold right out of the refrigerator. Just keep in mind, the larger the roast, the longer it will take to cook.

GF DF

6 garlic cloves, minced

2 tablespoons whole-grain Dijon mustard

2 tablespoons sea salt, plus a pinch, divided

2 tablespoons freshly ground black pepper, plus a pinch, divided

1 tablespoon dried thyme

¼ cup extra-virgin olive oil, plus 3 tablespoons, divided

1 (4-pound) boneless prime rib roast beef

1½ pounds baby or new potatoes, halved

½ pound beets, peeled and sliced

½ pound turnips, peeled and sliced

½ pound parsnips, peeled and sliced

1 Preheat the oven to 325°F.

2 In a small bowl, combine the garlic, mustard, 2 tablespoons of salt, 2 tablespoons of pepper, thyme, and ¼ cup of olive oil to create a rub. Spread the rub evenly over the prime rib, patting it well. Place the roast in the Dutch oven, fat-side up.

3 In a bowl, toss the potatoes, beets, turnips, and parsnips with the remaining 3 tablespoons olive oil, the remaining salt and pepper. Arrange the vegetables around the prime rib.

4 Cover the pot, place in the heated oven, and roast for about 20 minutes per pound for medium-rare, or until the internal temperature reaches 130°F. If you prefer a medium roast, take it out at 150°F. Let the roast rest for 20 minutes before carving to seal in the juices.

COOKING TIP: *Roasts should be close to room temperature before they go in the oven, to ensure even cooking. Take the roast out of the refrigerator at least 30 minutes prior to cooking.*

STUFFED MEATBALLS

SERVES 6 TO 8 PREP TIME: 10 MINUTES COOK TIME: 6 HOURS

Kids will adore these Greek-inspired meatballs with a surprise on the inside: gooey feta cheese. The combination of ground beef and ground lamb in this recipe enriches both the taste and texture. This meal is perfectly complemented by a starchy side dish to soak up the aromatic juices. Serve with orzo pasta, rice, mashed potatoes, or a basket of freshly baked bread for a wickedly tasty lunch or dinner.

1 egg, lightly beaten
½ cup seasoned bread crumbs
¼ cup chopped fresh parsley
2 cloves garlic, minced
Salt
Freshly ground black pepper
½ pound ground beef
½ pound ground lamb
3 ounces feta cheese, cut into ½-inch cubes
1 (8-ounce) can tomato sauce

1 Preheat the oven to 350°F.

2 In a large bowl, combine the egg, bread crumbs, parsley, and garlic, and season with salt and pepper. Add the ground beef and ground lamb. Mix well.

3 To make the meatballs, shape some of the meat mixture into a ball around a cheese cube, being sure to completely enclose the cheese.

4 Place the meatballs in a Dutch oven, cover, and bake in the heated oven for 20 minutes. Drain off the fat.

5 Pour the tomato sauce over the meatballs, and gently toss to coat. Return to the oven and cook for 45 minutes to 1 hour.

COOKING TIP: *To amp up the flavor of this dish, make your own tomato sauce. In the Dutch oven, heat 1 tablespoon of olive oil over medium heat. Add 1 chopped onion and 1 minced clove of garlic, and cook until the onion is tender. Stir in an 8-ounce can of tomato sauce, ¼ cup of beef broth or stock, and 1 teaspoon of crushed dried oregano. Heat through.*

LAMB SHANKS WITH VEGETABLES

SERVES 4 TO 6 PREP TIME: 10 MINUTES COOK TIME: 3 HOURS

The Dutch oven is ideal for slow-cooked dishes, such as these lamb shanks with vegetables. Braised slowly, the meat will be incredibly tender. Serve with buttered egg noodles, mashed potatoes, or creamy polenta.

GF **DF**

4 lamb shanks
Salt
Freshly ground black pepper
2 tablespoons extra-virgin olive oil
2 onions, chopped
2 carrots, chopped
2 parsnips, chopped
1 (28-ounce) can whole Italian plum tomatoes
1 cup chicken broth or stock
1 cup beef broth or stock
1 can chickpeas, drained and rinsed
1 teaspoon dried thyme
Parsley, for garnish

1 Season the lamb shanks with salt and pepper.

2 In a Dutch oven over medium-high heat, heat the olive oil. Brown the shanks, two at a time, about 2 minutes per side. Remove to a platter as they finish browning.

3 Add the onions, carrots, and parsnips to the pot, and sauté over medium heat for 5 to 7 minutes, or until lightly browned.

4 Increase the heat to medium-high. Add the tomatoes, chicken broth, beef broth, chickpeas and thyme. Bring to a boil.

5 Return the shanks to the pot. Briefly bring back to a boil, then cover and reduce the heat to low. Simmer for about 2½ hours, or until the meat is tender.

6 Remove the lid, increase the heat to medium-high, and cook about 10 minutes, or until the juices thicken. Garnish with fresh parsley and serve.

> **INGREDIENT TIP:** *Found at the lower section of the leg, lamb shanks are a full-flavored but tough cut of meat—making them perfect for slow, gentle braising in an aromatic sauce. The hours-long cooking transforms them into moist, fork-tender meat. Browning them first in olive oil gives them a nice color and enhances the taste.*

SHEPHERD'S PIE

SERVES 6 PREP TIME: 10 MINUTES COOK TIME: 1¼ TO 1¾ HOURS

You'll love the convenience of this English pub favorite. A meat pie with a crust of mashed potatoes, it's protein rich and appetizing. We've used ground lamb (the traditional recipe), but ground beef works equally well—just make sure to use beef broth or stock instead of chicken. To add an extra kick to the crust, sprinkle with grated Cheddar cheese before browning in the oven.

GF **DF**

1 (16-ounce) package frozen mixed vegetables
2 pounds ground lamb
1 cup chicken or beef broth or stock
1 tablespoon tomato paste
1 tablespoon Worcestershire sauce, or A.1. steak sauce
2 cloves garlic, minced
1 teaspoon crushed dried thyme
Salt
Freshly ground black pepper
1 (32-ounce) package refrigerated mashed potatoes

---

1 Preheat the oven to 325°F

2 Place the frozen vegetables in a Dutch oven. Add the ground lamb, broth, tomato paste, Worcestershire sauce, garlic, thyme, salt,

and pepper. Stir.

3 Cover, place in the heated oven, and cook for 1 to 1½ hours.

4 Remove the pot from the oven, and lower the temperature to 350°F. While the oven is heating, spoon the mashed potatoes into small mounds on top of the meat mixture. Smooth the surface with the back of the spoon.

5 Return the pot to the oven, uncovered, and bake for 15 minutes, or until the potatoes are slightly browned.

> **NUTRITION TIP:** *This recipe calls for frozen mixed vegetables and refrigerated mashed potatoes, which makes it quick and easy to prepare. If you'd like to up the nutritional goodness, use fresh veggies instead.*

LAMB CURRY

SERVES 6 PREP TIME: 15 MINUTES COOK TIME: 1½ HOURS

Curry is an easy and spicy option when it comes to slow-cooking lamb. Even the toughest pieces of meat are rendered juicy and succulent, thanks to the lengthy stewing time. Serve over a bed of rice, and your family will be fully satisfied—and full of compliments!

GF DF

2 tablespoons extra-virgin olive oil
3 pounds lamb stew meat, trimmed, and cut into 1-inch cubes
2 onions, chopped
4 cloves garlic, minced
2 tablespoons curry powder
1 teaspoon ground coriander
1 teaspoon ground cumin
Salt
Freshly ground black pepper
2 cups chicken broth or stock

1 In a Dutch oven over medium-high heat, heat the olive oil. Working in batches, cook the lamb pieces until browned on all sides, then transfer them to a platter.

2 Add the onions and garlic to the pot, and cook until translucent. Reduce the heat to medium, and add the curry powder, coriander,

cumin, salt, and pepper. Cook for about 3 minutes, stirring occasionally.

3 Return the meat to the pot, and pour in the broth. Bring to a boil, reduce to a simmer, and cook, uncovered, for about 1¼ hours.

> **COOKING TIP:** *To give this dish a more pronounced Eastern accent, serve over a bed of basmati rice. Garnish with a dollop of plain yogurt and chopped fresh cilantro.*

BRAISED ROSEMARY LAMB SHANKS

SERVES 6 TO 8 PREP TIME: 20 MINUTES COOK TIME: 3 TO 3½ HOURS

It's hard to beat this dish in terms of ease of preparation, succulence, and heartwarming appeal on a chilly fall evening. Aside from a quick initial browning, the cooking is practically unsupervised. Meanwhile, your kitchen will be alive with alluring aromas, and you'll be free to host your guests in style. Serving from the Dutch oven means the food stays hot and cleanup is a breeze.

GF DF

6 lamb shanks
Sea salt
Freshly ground black pepper
2 tablespoons extra-virgin olive oil
2 onions, chopped
3 carrots, chopped
10 cloves garlic, chopped
2 cups red wine
1 (28-ounce) can whole tomatoes
2 cups chicken broth or stock
1 cup beef broth or stock
1½ tablespoons chopped fresh rosemary (or 1 teaspoon dried rosemary)
2 teaspoons chopped fresh thyme (or 1 teaspoon dried thyme)

1 Preheat the oven to 325°F.

2 Season the lamb shanks with salt and pepper.

3 In a Dutch oven over medium-high heat, add the olive oil. When the oil is shimmering, add the shanks and cook until evenly browned, about 2 minutes per side. Transfer to a platter.

4 Return the pot to the stove over medium heat. Add the onions, carrots, and garlic. Cook for 5 to 7 minutes, or until the onions are browned. Increase the heat to high, and stir in the wine, scraping the bottom and sides of the pot with a wooden spoon to loosen any browned bits. Bring to a boil and add the tomatoes, chicken broth, beef broth, rosemary, and thyme. Return the shanks to the pot, and bring to a boil.

5 Cover, place in the preheated heated oven, and cook for about 2½ hours, or until the meat is tender.

6 Return the pot to the stove top, remove the cover, and cook for 30 to 40 minutes over medium-high heat, or until the sauce thickens.

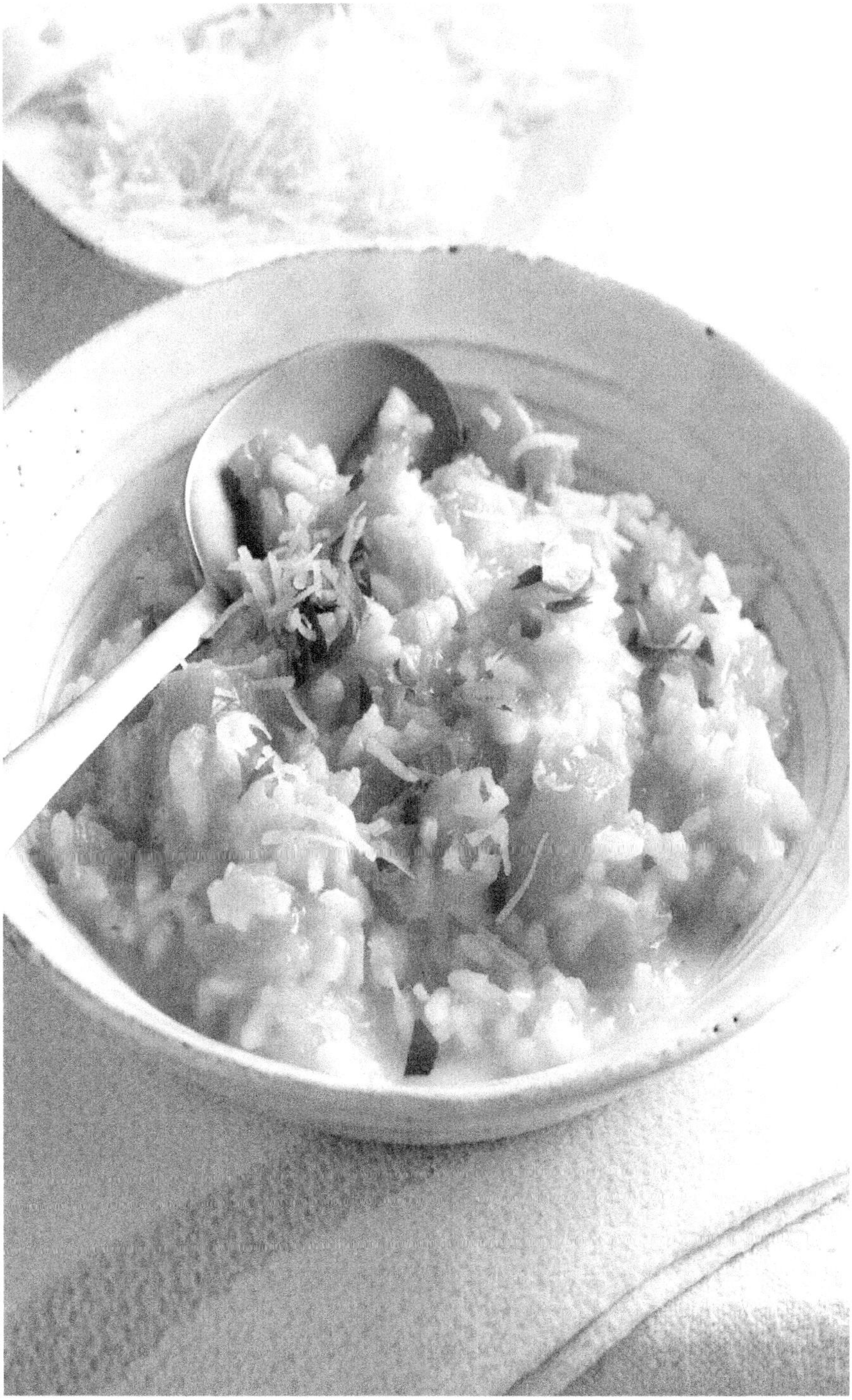

CHAPTER 7
MEATLESS MAINS

VEGETABLE BAKE

MEDITERRANEAN CHEESE TART

BUTTERNUT SQUASH RISOTTO

MUSHROOM RISOTTO

PUTTANESCA PASTA BAKE

VEGETABLE STIR-FRY

EGGS PIPERADE

WARM FARRO SALAD

KALE & SQUASH LASAGNA

VEGETABLE POLENTA CASSEROLE

WILD MUSHROOM PASTA BAKE

RUSTIC PIZZA

CHEESE FONDUE

SQUASH CASSEROLE

MEDLEY OF MUSHROOM STROGANOFF

GREEN BEAN CASSEROLE

VEGETABLE BAKE

SERVES 6 PREP TIME: 20 MINUTES COOK TIME: 1 HOUR

Spring: a time of new beginnings. And just in time, too—not only are the days getting longer and the temperatures rising—new spring vegetables show up to tantalize taste buds and get rid of the last of the winter blues. Although you can enjoy any vegetable year-round thanks to freezers and cans, nothing beats this dish's fresh-from-the-garden goodness.

GF DF V

1 pound red potatoes, halved
½ pound carrots, sliced
½ pound beets, sliced
1 shallot, peeled and sliced
10 cloves garlic, peeled and sliced
¼ cup balsamic vinegar
2 tablespoons extra-virgin olive oil
½ cup vegetable broth or stock
Salt
Freshly ground black pepper
½ cup chopped fresh basil leaves, divided
1 cup frozen peas

1 Preheat the oven to 400°F.

2 In a Dutch oven, combine the potatoes, carrots, beets, shallot, and garlic. Add the vinegar, olive oil, and broth. Season with salt and pepper, and sprinkle with ¼ cup of basil. Stir to combine.

3 Cover, place in the preheated oven, and bake for 50 minutes to 1 hour, or until the potatoes and carrots are lightly browned. After about 45 minutes, add the peas.

4 Remove from the oven, and season with more salt and pepper, if desired. Stir in the remaining ¼ cup basil, and serve in the Dutch oven.

STORAGE TIP: *To prolong the life of your fresh spring vegetables, store carrots, beets, and herbs (such as basil) in an unsealed plastic bag or in a paper towel in your refrigerator's crisper drawer. Potatoes, shallots, and garlic should be stored in a cool, dark pantry.*

MEDITERRANEAN CHEESE TART

SERVES 6 TO 8 PREP TIME: 40 MINUTES COOK TIME: 30 MINUTES

Using a Dutch oven for baking a tart might not seem like a match made in culinary heaven, but the top quality of cast-iron cooking, combined with the circular shape, works surprisingly well. Feel free to substitute any leftover veggies you might have on hand.

V | **30**

8 ounces frozen pie crust, thawed

3 ounces roasted red peppers in oil, drained and diced

6 ounces canned artichoke hearts, drained and quartered

1 ounce sun-dried tomatoes in oil, drained and chopped

½ teaspoon dried sage

½ teaspoon dried oregano

Salt

Freshly ground black pepper

3 eggs

½ cup low-fat milk

4 ounces feta cheese, crumbled

1 Preheat the oven to 350°F.

2 Roll out the pie crust to line the base and sides of the pot. Press into the pot, and refrigerate for 30 minutes.

3 In a bowl, mix together the red peppers, artichoke hearts, sun-dried tomatoes, sage, and oregano. Season with salt and pepper. Transfer to the pastry-lined pot. In the same bowl, beat together the eggs, milk, and cheese. Pour the egg mixture over the filling.

4 Cover, place in the preheated oven, and bake for 15 minutes. Remove and uncover. Lower the temperature to 300°F, return the pot to the oven, and continue baking for 10 to 15 minutes, or until the filling is set and the top is golden brown.

> **COOKING TIP:** *Allow the pot to cool for 10 to 15 minutes after removing it from the oven. Use a plastic spatula to gently ease the tart out of the pot, and slide it on to a warmed plate. Serve immediately.*

BUTTERNUT SQUASH RISOTTO

SERVES 8 PREP TIME: 10 MINUTES COOK TIME: 60 MINUTES

Risotto requires a lot of stirring, but the effort is well worth it. The constant stirring and the addition of liquid in small amounts releases the starch in the special arborio rice, making the risotto creamy and delicious.

5 tablespoons olive oil, divided
½ a butternut squash, peeled, seeded, and cut into ¼-inch pieces
1 teaspoon sea salt, divided
½ teaspoon freshly cracked black pepper, divided
1 onion, diced
1½ cups arborio rice
½ cup dry white wine
5½ cups chicken broth
2 tablespoons heavy cream
1 cup Parmesan cheese, grated, plus more for serving
2 tablespoons basil, cut into chiffonade

1 In a large Dutch oven over medium-high heat, put 3 tablespoons of the olive oil.

2 When the oil is shimmering, add the squash. Season it with ½ teaspoon of the salt and ¼ teaspoon of the pepper.

3 Cook the squash, stirring occasionally, for 6 to 8 minutes, until it is soft and starts to brown.

4 Remove the squash from the pot and set it aside on a plate.

5 Add the remaining 2 tablespoons olive oil to the pot, and heat it until it shimmers.

6 Add the onion and cook, stirring frequently, until the onion is soft, about 5 minutes.

7 Add the rice and cook, stirring constantly, for 1 minute.

8 Add the white wine and cook, stirring constantly, scraping all of the browned bits from the bottom of the pot with a wooden spoon. Continue cooking and stirring until the liquid has been absorbed.

9 Start adding the broth to the pot, a ladleful at a time, stirring constantly. Add the next ladleful only when the liquid has been absorbed from the previous addition. Continue working this way, stirring constantly, until all of the broth has been absorbed.

10 Reduce the heat to medium-low. Stir in the heavy cream, Parmesan cheese, and remaining ½ teaspoon salt and ¼ teaspoon pepper.

11 Stir in the reserved butternut squash. Cook, stirring frequently, for 3 to 4 minutes until the squash is warmed through.

12 Serve topped with chopped basil and Parmesan cheese.

PREPARATION TIP: *To cut the basil into chiffonade, lay several basil leaves in a stack. Roll the stack of leaves crosswise, and then cut the roll into thin strips.*

MUSHROOM RISOTTO

SERVES 6 PREP TIME: 15 MINUTES COOK TIME: 30 MINUTES

Risotto originated in northern Italy, where it is typically served as a first course (oftentimes as part of a six-course meal!). This recipe, enhanced with an exotic mushroom blend, creates a full-fledged, mouthwatering main course.

GF V 30

5 tablespoons unsalted butter
3 cups assorted fresh mushrooms (such as button, cremini, portobello, or oyster)
4 shallots, finely chopped
2 cloves garlic, minced
2½ cups arborio rice
1 cup dry white wine
Salt
Freshly ground black pepper
8 cups vegetable broth or stock
1 cup frozen peas, thawed
½ cup grated Asiago cheese, for garnish
½ cup fresh chopped parsley, for garnish

1 In a Dutch oven, heat the butter over medium-low heat until melted. Add the mushrooms, shallots, and garlic. Cook for 5 to 7

minutes, or until the mushrooms are lightly browned, stirring occasionally.

2 Add the rice to the pot, and stir until all the grains are coated with butter and the rice changes color slightly, about 2 minutes. Stir in the wine and season with salt and pepper.

3 Start adding the broth to the pot, a ladleful at a time, stirring constantly. Add another ladleful of broth only when the previous ladleful has been absorbed.

4 Continue cooking and adding more broth until the rice is creamy. Stir in the peas.

5 Serve, passing the cheese and parsley for garnish.

> **INGREDIENT TIP:** *Arborio is the most common type of rice that will produce an authentic risotto. It's a variety of short-grain rice that's particularly short and plump. Because it contains a very high starch content, it creates a creamy texture as it cooks. You'll know the risotto is done when you are able to flatten a grain of rice between your fingers.*

PUTTANESCA PASTA BAKE

SERVES 6 PREP TIME: 20 MINUTES COOK TIME: 25 MINUTES

Spicy puttanesca flavor (tomatoes, olives, and garlic) meets melty au gratin texture in this crowd-pleasing pasta dish. With just enough spice from the cayenne powder, and a salty boost from the Kalamata olives, this pasta combines the best Mediterranean flavors in one melt-in-your-mouth dish, all in under 30 minutes.

V | 30

12 ounces penne pasta (or any hollow pasta shape)

1 tablespoon extra-virgin olive oil

3 garlic cloves, minced

½ teaspoon cayenne powder

1 (14-ounce) can diced tomatoes

⅓ cup pitted and chopped Kalamata olives (or any cured black olives)

2 tablespoons chopped fresh parsley

2 tablespoons chopped fresh basil leaves

Salt

Freshly ground black pepper

1 cup grated mozzarella cheese, divided

¼ cup grated Parmesan cheese

1 Preheat the oven to 375°F.

2 In a Dutch oven over medium-high heat, bring salted water to a boil. Add the pasta and cook according to package directions until just barely al dente. Drain the pasta in a colander, and rinse quickly with cool water to stop cooking, and to remove excess starch. Set the rinsed pasta aside.

3 Heat the olive oil in the Dutch oven over medium-low heat. Add the garlic and cayenne powder, and sauté for about 30 seconds. Add the tomatoes and reduce heat to low. Simmer, stirring occasionally, for 5 to 10 minutes, or until the sauce is slightly thickened. Add the olives, parsley, and basil leaves. Season with salt and pepper.

4 Fold in the pasta and about ¾ cup of mozzarella cheese. Top with the remaining ¼ cup of mozzarella and the Parmesan. Cover, place in the heated oven, and bake for 15 minutes, or until the cheese melts and bubbles.

SUBSTITUTION TIP: *If you want to turn up the protein and dim down the dairy, swap smoked tofu for the mozzarella cheese. You can also sprinkle shredded nondairy cheese on top in place of Parmesan—Daiya that melts as well as the real thing.*

VEGETABLE STIR-FRY

SERVES 4 TO 6 PREP TIME: 20 MINUTES COOK TIME: 20 MINUTES

This stir-fry is a great way to give veggies a delectable do-over, thanks to the addition of ginger, lime juice, and garlic. Serve over brown rice for a protein-packed midweek meal, and sprinkle with sesame seeds to add a tasty, nutty crunch.

DF **V** **30**

⅓ cup extra-virgin olive oil

⅓ cup soy sauce

Juice of 1 lime

3 cloves garlic, minced

2 teaspoons freshly grated ginger

3 carrots, peeled and chopped

2 cups broccoli florets

1 red bell pepper, sliced

1 orange bell pepper, sliced

1 yellow bell pepper, sliced

1 red onion, sliced

6 ounces mushrooms

1 cup fresh or frozen snow peas

1 In a large bowl, combine the olive oil, soy sauce, lime juice, garlic, and ginger.

2 Add the carrots, broccoli, peppers, onion, mushrooms, and snow peas, and toss until they're coated with the oil mixture.

3 Heat the Dutch oven over medium heat. Add the vegetable mixture and cook for 20 minutes, or just until the vegetables are tender.

EGGS PIPÉRADE

SERVES 4 TO 6 PREP TIME: 15 MINUTES COOK TIME: 30 MINUTES

Eggs pipérade is a famous dish native to France's Basque region. It's an uncomplicated stew of peppers, tomatoes, and onions, with eggs added at the end to give it a frittata-like consistency. For a deliciously indulgent twist, swap 2 tablespoons of the olive oil with bacon, duck, or chicken fat. Try garnishing with some shredded fresh basil leaves.

GF DF V 30

- 4 tablespoons extra-virgin olive oil
- 2 onions, peeled and sliced
- 5 red bell peppers, seeded and sliced
- 5 fresh tomatoes, skinned, seeded, and chopped
- 2 garlic cloves, minced
- 1 tablespoon chopped fresh basil leaves (or 1 teaspoon dried basil)
- Salt
- Freshly ground black pepper
- 8 eggs

1 In a Dutch oven over medium-high heat, heat the olive oil. Reduce the heat to low, and sauté the onions until golden. Add the bell peppers and sauté until softened. Add the tomatoes, garlic, and

basil, and season with salt and pepper. Cook until the tomatoes disintegrate and the mixture takes on a purée-like consistency.

2 In a medium bowl, beat the eggs with salt and pepper. Pour the eggs over the vegetables. Cook for 3 to 5 minutes, until the eggs are set, stirring occasionally for a scrambled consistency. Remove the pot from the heat while the eggs are still moist and slightly undercooked. The residual heat will finish cooking them.

> **COOKING TIP:** *Cooking the peppers with the skin on makes for a crunchier dish. However, some prefer to peel them. The easiest way to do this is to use a sharp vegetable peeler in a sawing motion to remove the skin. Try the same method for the tomatoes, or plunge them into boiling water for a few seconds, and use a sharp knife to easily peel away the skin.*

WARM FARRO SALAD

SERVES 4 TO 6 PREP TIME: 10 MINUTES COOK TIME: 15 MINUTES

Farro is one of the oldest forms of wheat. It's been dated back to biblical times, and is still widely used in Europe. It looks like a plumper version of barley and can be used in stews, as a substitute for rice, or in salads—such as this one. Tomatoes, spinach, and feta round out this Mediterranean medley.

V **30**

1½ cups farro

1 (10- to 12-ounce) container grape tomatoes, halved

½ red onion, chopped

2 cups baby spinach

½ cup extra-virgin olive oil

¼ cup white wine vinegar

Salt

Freshly ground black pepper

6 ounces feta, crumbled

6 tablespoons chopped fresh basil leaves

1 Bring 5 cups of water to boil in a Dutch oven, add the farro, and cook for 10 to 15 minutes, or just until tender. Drain the water, leaving the farro in the pot.

2 While the pot is still warm, add the tomatoes, onion, and spinach to the pot, stirring to wilt the spinach leaves.

3 In a small bowl, whisk together the olive oil and vinegar. Season with salt and pepper, and add to the farro salad, along with the feta and basil. Toss everything together until all ingredients are evenly coated.

COOKING TIP: *This dish can be served warm or cold. The beauty of the Dutch oven is that it's adept at retaining either temperature during serving time. Plus, it makes a beautiful centerpiece.*

KALE & SQUASH LASAGNA

SERVES 4 TO 6 PREP TIME: 20 MINUTES COOK TIME: 30 MINUTES

This "garden-variety" lasagna sacrifices none of the decadence, richness, or tastiness of the classic meat recipe while remaining entirely friendly to vegetarian diets. Kale is rich in protein, fiber, and vitamins A, C, and K, while butternut squash is a fantastic source of immune-system-boosting omega-3s and beta-carotene.

V | **30**

3 cups diced butternut squash

4 cups chopped kale

2 yellow onions, diced

4 tablespoons extra-virgin olive oil, divided

Salt

Freshly ground black pepper

30 ounces ricotta cheese

2 eggs

1 tablespoon chopped fresh thyme (or ½ tablespoon dried)

2 (16-ounce) packages whole-wheat lasagna noodles, cooked according to directions

2 cups shredded mozzarella cheese

1 Preheat the oven to 400°F.

2 In a Dutch oven, combine the butternut squash, kale, and onions. Toss with 3 tablespoons of olive oil, and season with salt and

pepper. Cover, place in the preheated oven, and roast for 10 to 20 minutes, or until the squash is tender. Transfer the squash to a platter.

3 In a medium bowl, combine the ricotta cheese, eggs, and thyme.

4 Brush the Dutch oven with the remaining 1 tablespoon olive oil. Line the bottom with a layer of lasagna noodles. Add ¼ of the ricotta and ¼ of the squash mixture, and ⅕ of the mozzarella cheese. Repeat 4 times, topping the final layer of lasagna noodles with the remaining mozzarella. Return the pot to the oven and bake for 10 to 15 minutes, or until the cheese is golden and bubbly.

> **SUBSTITUTION TIP:** *Some palates are not fond of ricotta cheese, or its common substitute, cottage cheese. Consider swapping in more imaginative alternatives, such as goat cheese, silken tofu, or puréed cauliflower.*

VEGETABLE POLENTA CASSEROLE

SERVES 6 TO 8 PREP TIME: 20 MINUTES COOK TIME: 1 TO 1½ HOURS

Polenta is becoming increasingly popular and for good reason. Cornmeal is full of fiber and is gluten-free, and when prepared as polenta is extremely versatile as well as hearty. For dinner, serve it as a substitute for mashed potatoes, or use it as a base on which to ladle any number of savory sauces. In this recipe, it is the basis of a melt-in-your-mouth, cheesy bean casserole.

GF V

2 (19-ounce) cans white kidney beans, rinsed and drained
1 (19-ounce) can garbanzo beans, rinsed and drained
1 cup chopped onion
4 cloves garlic, minced
1 teaspoon crushed dried thyme
1 teaspoon crushed dried oregano
1 (16-ounce) tube refrigerated cooked polenta, cut into ½-inch slices
2 cups shredded assorted Italian cheeses (your choice of Provolone, mozzarella, Parmesan, Romano, fontina, or Asiago)
1 large tomato, sliced
2 cups fresh spinach leaves

1 Preheat the oven to 325°F.

2 In a large bowl, combine the kidney beans, garbanzo beans, onion, garlic, thyme, and oregano.

3 In the Dutch oven, layer half of the bean mixture, half of the polenta, and half of the cheeses. Add the remaining bean mixture and the remaining polenta.

4 Cover, place in the preheated oven, and cook for 1 to 1½ hours.

5 Remove the pot from the oven. Uncover and sprinkle the remaining cheeses on top. Add the tomato and spinach, toss lightly, and serve.

> **INGREDIENT TIP:** *A type of cornmeal, polenta can be found in most grocery stores. It's usually sold in its dry form, although you can buy it already cooked, which is what we've used here. Make sure to store precooked polenta in a cool, dry place. If you buy dry polenta instead, keep it in the refrigerator once it's been cooked. If you cannot find polenta, regular yellow cornmeal or grits will substitute perfectly.*

WILD MUSHROOM PASTA BAKE

SERVES 4 TO 6 ■ PREP TIME: 20 MINUTES ■ COOK TIME: 1 HOUR

This creamy casserole will warm hearts and fill bellies on a cold autumn's eve. A Parmesan, thyme, and bread crumb crust adds a delightfully crunchy texture and a savory taste. For an extra-rich dose of flavor, add two tablespoons of sherry to the mushrooms and onions while sautéing.

V

4 tablespoons butter, divided
1 onion, chopped
1 pound wild mushrooms, chopped
3 tablespoons chopped fresh thyme, divided
Salt
Freshly ground black pepper
1 tablespoon flour
1 cup whole milk
½ cup heavy cream
12 ounces shredded Gruyère cheese
4 cups penne pasta, cooked al dente
2 cups baby spinach, torn into bite-size pieces
1¼ cups bread crumbs
3 tablespoons grated Parmesan cheese

1 Preheat the oven to 325°F.

2 In a Dutch oven on medium, melt 2 tablespoons butter. Add the onion and mushrooms, and cook until the mushrooms are just tender, for 4 to 5 minutes. Add 2 tablespoons of thyme, and season with salt and pepper. Transfer to a large bowl.

3 In the Dutch oven, melt the remaining 2 tablespoons butter. Whisk in the flour and cook for about 1 minute. Gradually add the milk and cream, and cook until the milk begins to thicken, whisking continuously. Remove the pot from the heat. Stir in the Gruyère cheese until it melts.

4 Add the cooked pasta and spinach to the mushroom mixture. Stir. Return the mushroom mixture to the Dutch oven, and fold into the cheese sauce.

5 Cover, place in the heated oven, and bake for 20 minutes.

6 In a small bowl, combine the bread crumbs, the remaining 1 tablespoon thyme, and the Parmesan cheese.

7 Remove the pasta from the oven, and sprinkle the bread crumb mixture on top. Increase the oven temperature to 375°F, and bake for 15 to 20 minutes, uncovered, until the crust is golden.

> **NUTRITION TIP:** *From shiitake to chanterelle, morel to maitake, reishi to porcini, every species of wild mushroom has its own unique flavor. But they share one common trait: an extraordinarily high medicinal value. The compounds contained in maitake, for example, have the capacity not only to stimulate immune function but also to inhibit tumor growth, which is why Chinese herbalists have been using mushrooms for remedies and cures for more than three thousand years.*

RUSTIC PIZZA

SERVES 4 TO 6 PREP TIME: 10 MINUTES COOK TIME: 20 TO 30 MINUTES

This traditional pizza recipe is unbelievably easy, fast, and tasty. The whole family will be clamoring for more! And the best part is, with two super fresh ingredients, it's incredibly clean and healthy.

V | **30**

1 (14-ounce) can refrigerated pizza crust dough

Extra-virgin olive oil, for greasing

2 plum tomatoes, stem ends removed, cut into ¼-inch slices, and salted

4 ounces grated mozzarella cheese

½ cup chopped fresh basil leaves, for garnish

1 Preheat the oven to 375°F.

2 Roll out the pizza crust dough, and trim to line the base of a Dutch oven. Wrap and freeze any extra dough.

3 Brush the bottom of the pot with olive oil. Place the crust in the pot.

4 Spread the sliced tomatoes over the dough, leaving a 1-inch rim at the edge. Cover with the cheese. Lightly brush the rim of the crust with olive oil, for a nice crispy finish.

5 Place the pot in the preheated oven, and cook for 20 to 30 minutes, or until the dough is cooked and the cheese is melted.

6 Transfer the pizza to a cutting board, and garnish with the basil.

COOKING TIP: *If you prefer your pizza with a little more sauce, purée a large (28-ounce) can of whole peeled tomatoes. Add 1 diced, sautéed onion, and bring to a simmer. Add 1 tablespoon of dried oregano, and season with salt and pepper. Spoon over the pizza crust dough, and top with the mozzarella cheese, as in the above recipe.*

CHEESE FONDUE

SERVES 6 TO 8 ■ PREP TIME: 15 MINUTES ■ COOK TIME: 1¼ TO 1¾ HOURS

Considered the national dish of Switzerland, fondue consists of melted cheese served in a communal pot over a small flame, which keeps the fondue mixture warm enough to stay smooth and liquid. The Dutch oven, with its inimitable heat-retaining ability, makes the perfect serving vessel. It's a real winner at the dinner table or at a cocktail party.

V

3 cups vegetable broth or stock
3 cups whipping cream
1 cup dry white wine
3 cloves garlic, minced
½ cup softened butter
½ cup all-purpose flour
1 tablespoon Dijon mustard
16 ounces shredded Gruyère cheese
8 ounces shredded Emmentaler cheese

1 Preheat the oven to 325°F.

2 In a Dutch oven, combine the broth, cream, wine, and garlic. Cover, place in the heated oven, and cook for 1 to 1½ hours.

3 In a medium bowl, stir together the butter and flour, until the mixture forms a paste. Whisk it into the broth mixture until completely incorporated. Cover the pot, return to the oven, and cook for 5 to 10 minutes, or until the mixture starts to thicken.

4 Blend the mustard into the broth mixture. Gradually stir in the Gruyère and the Emmentaler, until the cheese melts and the fondue becomes smooth. Serve with your choice of dippers.

> **COOKING TIP:** *Get creative with your dippers. The classic choice is French bread cubes. For a vitamin-rich twist, try steamed broccoli or cauliflower florets, chunks of roasted parsnip, boiled fingerling potatoes, or apple slices.*

SQUASH CASSEROLE

SERVES 6 PREP TIME: 30 MINUTES COOK TIME: 2 TO 2½ HOURS

Winter squash arrives late in the growing season and has a long shelf life, which makes it a staple in winter and spring, when many other vegetables are harder to come by. Unlike its summer counterpart, winter squash must be cooked. This fiber-rich variety is equally wonderful baked or steamed. And, owing to its dense and creamy texture, it makes a nourishing and heartwarming base to this spicy, pulse-racing casserole.

GF **V**

1½ cups peeled and chopped butternut squash
1½ cups peeled and chopped acorn squash
1 (15-ounce) can hominy, rinsed and drained
1 (15-ounce) can black beans, rinsed and drained
2 onions, chopped
2 red bell peppers, chopped
1 (4-ounce) can diced green chile peppers
1 cup tomato sauce
½ cup salsa
4 cloves garlic, minced
Salt
Freshly ground black pepper
½ cup shredded Monterey Jack cheese
Chopped fresh cilantro, for garnish

1 Preheat the oven to 325°F.

2 In a Dutch oven, combine the butternut squash, acorn squash, hominy, black beans, onions, red bell peppers, chile peppers, tomato sauce, salsa, and garlic. Season with salt and pepper.

3 Cover, place in the preheated oven, and bake for 2 to 2½ hours.

4 Sprinkle the cheese on top, garnish with the cilantro, and serve.

> **NUTRITION TIP:** *One of the most common winter squash, butternut squash boasts the highest doses of vitamins A and C. It has thin, butterscotch-colored skin, and sweet, nutty flesh. For the most abundant flesh, choose one with a long, thick neck. Shaped like its namesake, acorn squash is a small, dark-green squash with a moist yellow to orange interior that's loaded with fiber.*

MEDLEY OF MUSHROOM STROGANOFF

SERVES 4 TO 6 PREP TIME: 20 MINUTES COOK TIME: 10 MINUTES

Mushrooms replace beef in our vegetarian variation on the classic Russian dish. For enhanced impact and texture, combine at least three different types of fungi. You'll be astonished at how quick and easy it is to make this toothsome dish.

GF V 30

2 tablespoons extra-virgin olive oil
2 shallots, finely chopped
12 ounces assorted fresh mushrooms (such as shiitake, cremini, oyster, button, or portobello), chopped into bite-size pieces
¼ cup full-bodied red wine
2 tablespoons sour cream
2 teaspoons tomato paste
½ teaspoon Dijon mustard
Salt
Freshly ground black pepper

1 In a Dutch oven on medium-high, heat the olive oil. Add the shallots and gently sauté until softened but not browned.

2 Add the mushrooms and cook until they just begin to soften. Stir in the wine, sour cream, tomato paste, and mustard. Season with salt

and pepper. Cook, stirring, for 2 to 3 minutes, until the sauce heats and becomes smooth.

> **COOKING TIP:** *To round out this delectable but light fare, serve over brown rice or egg noodles, and garnish with fresh chopped parsley.*

GREEN BEAN CASSEROLE

SERVES 6 TO 8 PREP TIME: 20 MINUTES COOK TIME: 1 TO 1¼ HOURS

Smoked Gouda cheese and roasted red peppers add a delicious smokiness to this green bean casserole, while French-fried onions add a salty, crunchy kick. With minimal prep work and practically unsupervised cooking time, it's an easy dish to pull together for a midweek meal that's packed with nutrients and big on flavor.

V

1 pound fresh or frozen green beans

1 tablespoon extra-virgin olive oil

4 cups sliced mushrooms

3 cloves garlic, minced

1 (15-ounce) can condensed cream of mushroom soup

1 cup shredded smoked Gouda cheese

¼ cup milk

½ tablespoons whole-grain mustard

1 cup roasted red bell pepper strips

1 (10-ounce) can French-fried onions

Salt

Freshly ground black pepper

1 Preheat the oven to 325°F.

2 In a Dutch oven, cook the green beans in boiling salted water for 3 minutes. Drain and remove to a bowl.

3 Heat the olive oil in the Dutch oven over medium heat, and cook the mushrooms and the garlic until beginning to brown. Stir in the soup, cheese, milk, and mustard. Return the beans to the pot. Add the roasted peppers and the French-fried onions. Season with salt and pepper, and toss all the ingredients together.

4 Cover, place in the heated oven, and cook for 1 to 1¼ hours.

> **INGREDIENT TIP:** *Not only are green beans good for you, you can also enjoy this dish knowing you're supporting food sustainability in your own backyard. Although countries such as France, Mexico, and Argentina are large-scale producers of green beans, as much as 60 percent of all commercially grown green beans are produced in the United States. Just one more reason to enjoy this delicious vegetable.*

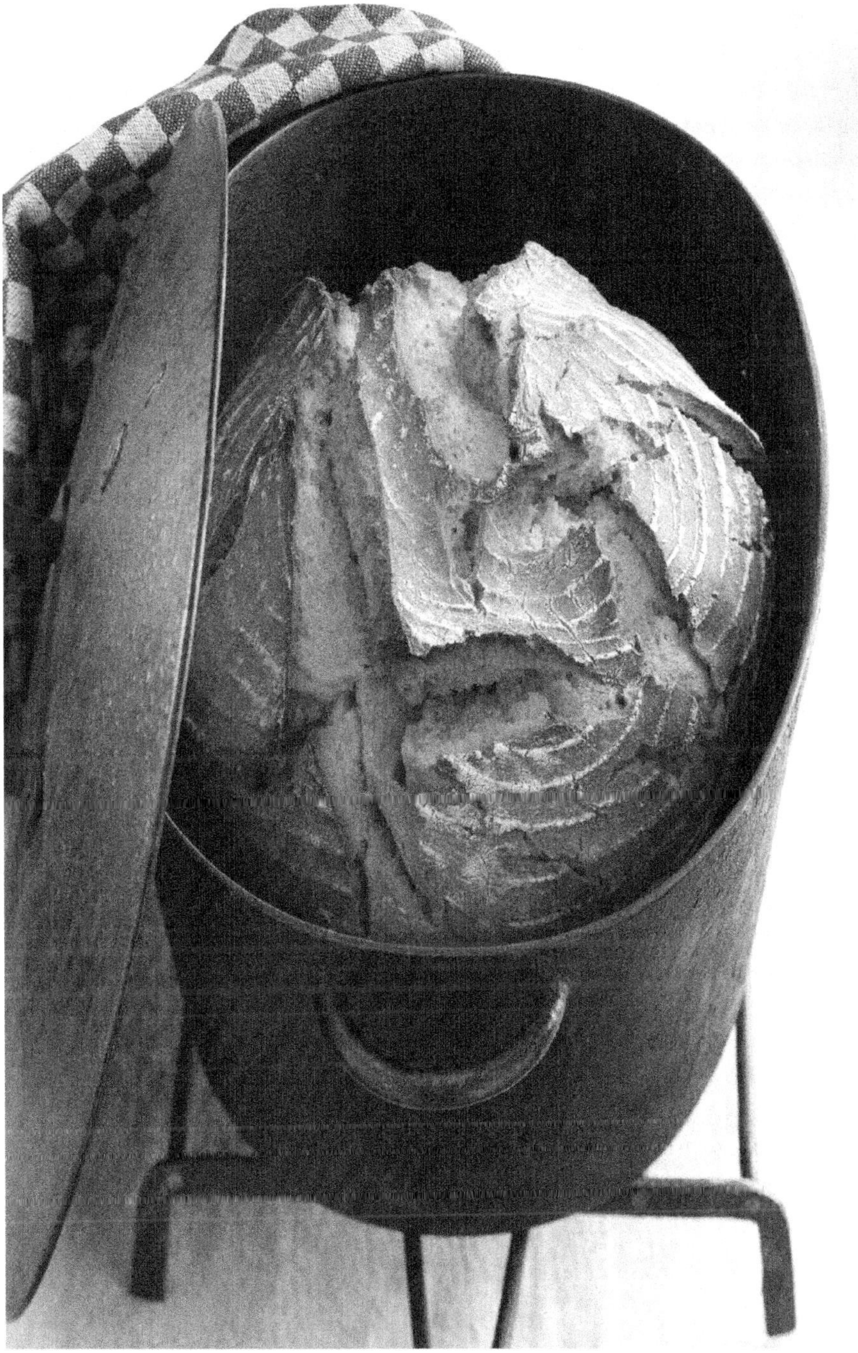

CHAPTER 8
BREADS & ROLLS

CLASSIC DUTCH OVEN BREAD

IRISH SODA BREAD

SAVORY CORNBREAD

PARMESAN OLIVE BREAD

IRISH SODA BREAD WITH ROSEMARY & GARLIC

PARMESAN ROSEMARY BREAD

JALAPEÑO CORNBREAD

LEMON BREAD

COCONUT BREAD

SEEDED DINNER ROLLS

CLASSIC DUTCH OVEN BREAD

MAKES 1 LOAF PREP TIME: 3 TO 5 HOURS COOK TIME: 1 HOUR

With just a handful of simple, wholesome ingredients, your Dutch oven can produce moist, melt-in-your-mouth bread that will prove a worthy accompaniment to just about any dish. Although this recipe seems to require a lot of prep time, most of it is simply allowing the dough enough time to rise—leaving you free to focus on other tasks.

DF | **V**

4 cups all-purpose flour
1½ cups water
1 teaspoon instant yeast
1½ teaspoons salt, divided (preferably kosher or sea salt)
Cooking spray
1 tablespoon extra-virgin olive oil

---

1 Combine the flour, water, yeast, and 1 teaspoon of salt in the bowl of a stand mixer. Using the dough hook attachment, knead on medium speed for 5 to 10 minutes, or until the dough is smooth and elastic.

2 Remove the bowl from the mixer, and cover it with plastic wrap. Let the dough rise from 2 to 4 hours, or until it has doubled in size.

3 Transfer the dough to a floured work surface, and knead it gently to release the gas and redistribute the yeast. Use your palms to

shape it into a tight ball.

4 Coat the bottom and sides of the Dutch oven with the cooking spray. Place the dough in the center of the pot and cover. Allow the dough to rise again for 40 to 50 minutes.

5 Preheat the oven to 450°F.

6 Brush the surface of the dough with olive oil. Using a sharp knife, score the top with ½-inch-deep overlapping cuts. Sprinkle with the remaining ½ teaspoon of salt. Cover, place in the oven, and bake for 30 minutes. Remove the lid, reduce the oven temperature to 375°F, and continue baking for 30 minutes, or until the bread is nicely browned.

> **INGREDIENT TIP:** *Yeast is what makes bread rise—just as baking soda and baking powder make your muffins and cakes rise. Because it has a smaller granule size, instant yeast dissolves faster than active dry yeast, which means you can mix it into your bread dough along with the rest of the dry ingredients.*

IRISH SODA BREAD

MAKES 1 LOAF ■ PREP TIME: 10 MINUTES ■ COOK TIME: 1 HOUR

Soda bread uses baking soda as a leavening agent instead of yeast. Traditional Irish loaves use whole-wheat flour, white flour, or both. The lactic acid in another key ingredient, sour milk, reacts with the baking soda to form tiny bubbles of carbon dioxide. In this recipe, oats add a crunchy texture to this timeless classic.

V

4 cups whole-wheat flour
1 cup white flour
½ cup rolled oats
1 teaspoon baking soda
2 teaspoons salt
2½ cups sour milk (or combine 2 tablespoons white vinegar with 2½ cups milk)
Cooking spray

---

1 Preheat the oven to 375°F.

2 In large bowl, mix the whole-wheat flour, white flour, rolled oats, baking soda, and salt. Add the sour milk and stir until the mixture is thoroughly moistened, forming a dough.

3 Place the dough on a floured surface and knead until smooth, about 5 minutes. Use floured hands to form the dough into a round.

Using a sharp knife, score a large, ½-inch-deep cross into the top.

4 Lightly coat the Dutch oven with cooking spray, and place the dough in the center. Cover, place in the heated oven, and bake for 1 hour, or until the bread is golden brown.

> **COOKING TIP:** *How can you tell when the bread is done? There are several ways of checking: (1) Tap the crust with your fingernail—if the bread sounds hollow, it's ready. (2) Insert a wooden toothpick near the center of the bread. If it comes out clean, it's fully baked. (3) Check the temperature—the dough should have an internal temperature of about 200°F.*

SAVORY CORNBREAD

MAKES 1 LOAF ■ PREP TIME: 30 MINUTES ■ COOK TIME: 20 TO 25 MINUTES

Corn has been cultivated for thousands of years by the indigenous people of the Americas, and prepared in as many different ways as there are cultures. When Europeans colonized North America, they adapted many of these techniques, and later incorporated them into their traditional European cookery. Cornbread as we know it really became popular during the Civil War, due to its low cost and versatility, lending itself to many different methods of on-the-go cooking. Today it's as much an American classic as ever, especially in the South and Southwest.

V | **30**

- 1¼ cups yellow cornmeal
- 1¼ cups all-purpose flour
- 2 tablespoons sugar
- 1¼ teaspoons baking powder
- ½ teaspoon baking soda
- 1¼ teaspoons salt (preferably kosher or sea salt)
- 1 large egg
- 1¾ cups buttermilk
- 1 cup grated Cheddar cheese
- ½ cup chopped scallions
- 3 tablespoons unsalted butter

1 Preheat the oven to 400°F.

2 In a large bowl, combine the cornmeal, flour, sugar, baking powder, baking soda, and salt.

3 In a separate bowl, whisk together the egg and the buttermilk. Stir the egg mixture into the flour mixture.

4 Add the cheese and scallions to the flour-and-egg mixture. Stir.

5 Melt the butter in the Dutch oven over medium heat, and swirl to coat the bottom and sides. Pour in the batter.

6 Cover, place in the oven, and bake for 20 to 25 minutes.

COOKING TIP: *The addition of cheese and scallions lifts this otherwise classic cornbread recipe up a notch, making it a finger-licking-good companion to rich, creamy chowders. Slice into thick wedges to serve.*

PARMESAN OLIVE BREAD

MAKES 1 LOAF ■ PREP TIME: 2½ TO 4½ HOURS ■ COOK TIME: 1 HOUR

Parmesan and olives give this homemade bread a salty, savory Mediterranean flavor. Although the prep time seems lengthy, most of it is simply to allow the dough sufficient time to rise. One of the optimum places for doing this, in terms of heat and humidity, is your oven—just be sure you haven't turned it on.

V

4 cups all-purpose flour
1 teaspoon instant yeast
1 teaspoon salt
1½ cups water, divided
1¼ cups grated Parmesan cheese, divided
¾ cup Kalamata olives, pitted and halved
Butter or cooking spray
1 teaspoon extra-virgin olive oil

1 Pour the flour, yeast, salt, and 1 cup of water into the base of a stand mixer. Using the bread hook attachment, mix briefly to combine the ingredients. Once combined, add the remaining ½ cup water, 1 cup grated cheese, and the olives. Mix until the dough is thoroughly combined.

2 Remove the bowl from the mixer, and cover it with plastic wrap. Let the dough rise until it has doubled in size, 2 to 4 hours.

3 When the dough is fully risen, preheat the oven to 450°F. Transfer the dough to a floured surface, and knead gently to release any gas. Use floured hands to form it into a round.

4 Grease the Dutch oven with butter or cooking spray. Place the dough in the center. Brush the top with olive oil, and sprinkle with the remaining ¼ cup cheese.

5 Cover, place in the heated oven, and bake for 30 minutes. Reduce the heat to 375°F, and bake until the bread is golden brown, about 30 minutes.

COOKING TIP: *Check that the knobs on your Dutch oven are oven-safe at 450°F. Stainless steel knobs should be fine, but some phenolic (a type of plastic or resin engineered to withstand high temperatures) knobs are oven-safe to only 375°F. If so, you'll need to remove the knob on yours when baking at temperatures in excess of this.*

IRISH SODA BREAD WITH ROSEMARY & GARLIC

MAKES 1 LOAF ▪ PREP TIME: 30 MINUTES ▪ COOK TIME: 35 TO 40 MINUTES

In nineteenth-century Ireland, soda bread was typically baked in a large, three-legged black iron pot over a turf fire—making it a perfect pairing for the Dutch oven. With the inclusion of garlic and rosemary, this artisanal loaf is an ideal companion for anything from a light summer salad to a hearty pasta dish.

V

2½ cups all-purpose flour
1 cup whole-wheat flour
1½ teaspoons baking soda
1 teaspoon salt
3 tablespoons sugar
1 teaspoon dried rosemary
3 garlic cloves, minced
1 cup buttermilk
1 large egg, beaten
3 tablespoons unsalted butter, melted
Cooking spray

1 Preheat the oven to 400°F.

2 In a large bowl, mix together the all-purpose flour, whole-wheat flour, baking soda, salt, and sugar. Add the rosemary and garlic. Stir.

3 In a small bowl, whisk together the buttermilk, egg, and melted butter.

4 Add the buttermilk mixture to the flour mixture, and stir with a wooden spoon until the dough has a sticky consistency.

5 Turn the dough onto a floured surface, and use your hands to shape it into a ball. Dust the top with flour. With a sharp knife, cut a ½-inch-deep cross into the top.

6 Lightly coat the Dutch oven with cooking spray. Place the dough in the center. Cover, place in the preheated oven, and bake for 20 minutes. Remove the lid and bake for 15 to 20 minutes, or until the top is golden brown.

> **COOKING TIP:** *Cutting crosses in the top of breads allow them to expand freely, and to form "ears"—raised flaps of crust at the edge of a cut.*

PARMESAN ROSEMARY BREAD

MAKES 1 LOAF ■ PREP TIME: 20 MINUTES ■ COOK TIME: 1 HOUR

You won't believe the flavor and moistness of this crusty, peasant-style loaf—or what a snap it is to make! It's ideal served with soups, stews, salads, or fresh pasta.

V

1½ cups warm water
1 package active dry yeast
3 cups all-purpose flour
3 tablespoons whole-wheat flour
½ cup finely shredded Parmesan cheese
1 tablespoon fresh rosemary, chopped
1½ teaspoons salt
Cooking spray

1 In a large bowl, whisk the warm water and the yeast together. Let stand for about 10 minutes, or until the mixture is foamy.

2 Add the all-purpose flour, whole-wheat flour, cheese, rosemary, and salt. Stir just until the mixture forms a ball, about 1 minute. Cover the bowl with plastic wrap, and let it stand until the dough doubles in size, 2 to 4 hours.

3 When dough has risen, preheat the oven to 400°F. Place the dough on a floured work surface, and use floured hands to shape it

into a ball.

4 Lightly coat the Dutch oven with cooking spray, and place the dough in the center.

5 Cover, place in the heated oven, and bake for 50 to 55 minutes. Remove the lid, return the pot to the oven, and bake for a few minutes, until the bread is golden.

> **INGREDIENT TIP:** *Unlike instant yeast, active dry yeast needs to be "activated" by adding it to water that's slightly warmer than lukewarm—110°F is ideal. It's usually sold in packets of three or four and should be stored at room temperature. Compared with instant yeast, it has a longer rise time that many bread bakers prefer: The longer fermentation time helps the bread develop more flavor.*

JALAPEÑO CORNBREAD

MAKES 1 LOAF PREP TIME: 20 MINUTES COOK TIME: 50 TO 60 MINUTES

Cornbread gets a spicy Southwestern makeover, thanks to the addition of chile peppers, onions, and scallions. It's the perfect accent to a bowl of smoking hot chili. And because cornbread tastes just as good the following day, you can use it to mop up leftovers.

V

1 cup yellow cornmeal
¾ cup all-purpose flour
¼ cup sugar
1 teaspoon baking powder
¾ teaspoon salt
2 eggs, lightly beaten
¾ cup milk
¼ cup vegetable oil
¼ cup finely chopped onion
¼ cup thinly sliced scallions
1 or 2 fresh jalapeño peppers, seeded and finely chopped
Cooking spray

1 Preheat the oven to 400°F.

2 In a medium bowl, combine the cornmeal, flour, sugar, baking powder, and salt.

3 In a small bowl, combine the eggs, milk, vegetable oil, onion, scallions, and jalapeño peppers. Add the egg mixture to the cornmeal mixture, and stir just until moistened.

4 Lightly coat the Dutch oven with cooking spray, and spoon the batter into the bottom.

5 Cover, place in the preheated oven, and bake for 50 minutes to 1 hour, or until a toothpick inserted near the center comes out clean.

> **STORAGE TIP:** *To store bread, cover with foil or plastic wrap, or place it in a plastic bag, so it doesn't dry out. Bread will stay fresh at room temperature for up to two days and will stay fresh in a refrigerator for a week. To freeze, wrap leftovers tightly in foil or plastic freezer wrap, or place in a heavy-duty freezer bag.*

LEMON BREAD

MAKES 1 LOAF PREP TIME: 10 MINUTES COOK TIME: 35 TO 40 MINUTES

No artificial fragrance could hold a candle to the natural lemony aroma emanating from your kitchen when baking this vibrant, citrusy bread. A generous amount of lemon juice and zest mixed into the batter lend this bread a bright liveliness. Meanwhile, poppy seeds add a crunchy texture and slightly nutty taste.

V

2 cups all-purpose flour

¼ **cup poppy seeds**

1 tablespoon baking powder

½ **teaspoon salt**

3 eggs, lightly beaten

1 cup sugar

½ **cup vegetable oil**

½ **cup sour cream**

¼ **cup milk**

1 teaspoon finely shredded lemon peel

¼ **cup lemon juice**

Butter, for greasing, or cooking spray

1 Preheat the oven to 400°F.

2 In a large bowl, combine the flour, poppy seeds, baking powder, and salt, and mix well.

3 In a small bowl, combine the eggs, sugar, vegetable oil, sour cream, milk, lemon peel, and lemon juice. Whisk together thoroughly, until the mixture becomes slightly creamy or pudding-like in texture.

4 Add the egg mixture to the flour mixture, and stir just until moistened.

5 Generously grease the Dutch oven with butter or coat it with cooking spray, and spoon the batter into the pot. Cover, place in the heated oven, and bake for 35 to 40 minutes, or until the top is slightly browned and springs back lightly when touched with a finger.

> **COOKING TIP:** *Once you remove the bread from the oven, allow it to cool for 10 to 15 minutes with the Dutch oven lid on. Run a plastic spatula around the rim of the Dutch oven to loosen the sides of the bread. Carefully empty it onto a wire rack, and allow the bread to cool completely.*

COCONUT BREAD

MAKES 1 LOAF ■ PREP TIME: 20 MINUTES ■ COOK TIME: 1 HOUR

What better way to usher in summer—and fragrance your kitchen and home—than with a succulent recipe ripe with the Caribbean flavors of coconut and lime? There's no need to book a flight when you whip up a loaf that's so deliciously moist, sweet, and transporting.

DF **V**

3 cups all-purpose flour

2 teaspoons baking powder

½ teaspoon salt

¾ cup flaked coconut

½ cup unsweetened coconut milk

1 cup cream of coconut

½ cup vegetable oil

3 egg whites

½ cup sugar

1 tablespoon finely chopped lime peel

¼ cup lime juice

Butter, for greasing, or cooking spray

1 Preheat the oven to 400°F.

2 In a large bowl, combine the flour, baking powder, salt, and flaked coconut.

3 In a medium bowl, combine the coconut milk, cream of coconut, vegetable oil, egg whites, sugar, lime peel, and lime juice. Add the coconut milk mixture to the flour mixture, and stir just until moistened.

4 Grease the Dutch oven with butter or coat it with cooking spray, and spoon the batter into the pot. Cover, place in the preheated oven, and bake for 1 hour, or until a wooden toothpick comes out clean.

> **INGREDIENT TIP:** *Cream of coconut is to coconut milk what condensed milk is to regular milk. It's made by skimming off the thick, rich layer of cream that forms on top of coconut milk. Though it has a rich, buttery texture and a delicious coconut taste, it's surprisingly not that sweet. You'll find it with the drink mixers in the liquor section of your supermarket or at your local liquor store.*

SEEDED DINNER ROLLS

MAKES 7 ROLLS ■ PREP TIME: 2¾ TO 3¾ HOURS ■ COOK TIME: 20 TO 25 MINUTES

Soft, sweet, and topped with a crunchy seed mixture, these rolls are sure to become a year-round favorite. Pass these around the table, and pair them with a hot bowl of soup, a creamy casserole, a fresh salad, or a light omelet.

V **30**

½ cup whole milk

3 tablespoons honey

¼ teaspoon sea salt

1½ teaspoons instant yeast

3 tablespoons cubed butter

1¾ cups all-purpose flour

Butter or cooking spray, for greasing

1 egg white, lightly beaten

1 teaspoon sesame seeds

1 teaspoon poppy seeds

1 teaspoon flaxseed

---

1 In a large bowl, combine the milk, honey, salt, and yeast. Add the butter and flour, and mix until the ingredients are well combined. Place onto a floured work surface. Knead the dough until it is soft and pliable but still a little sticky, about 5 minutes.

2 Transfer to a bowl. Cover with plastic wrap and let the dough rise for 2 to 3 hours, or until doubled in size.

3 Preheat the oven to 400°F. Generously butter a Dutch oven, or coat with cooking spray. Divide the dough into 7 equal pieces. Use floured hands to form each piece into a ball. Place 1 ball in the center of the Dutch oven, and space the other 6 balls evenly around it.

4 Brush the tops of the rolls with the egg white. Sprinkle generously with the sesame seeds, poppy seeds, and flaxseed. Cover and let stand until the rolls are slightly risen and puffy, about 30 minutes.

5 Place in the preheated oven, and bake for 20 to 25 minutes, or until the tops are golden.

STORAGE TIP: *To store yeast, transfer it to an airtight container (glass or acrylic), and keep it in the freezer, where it will stay fresh for up to a year.*

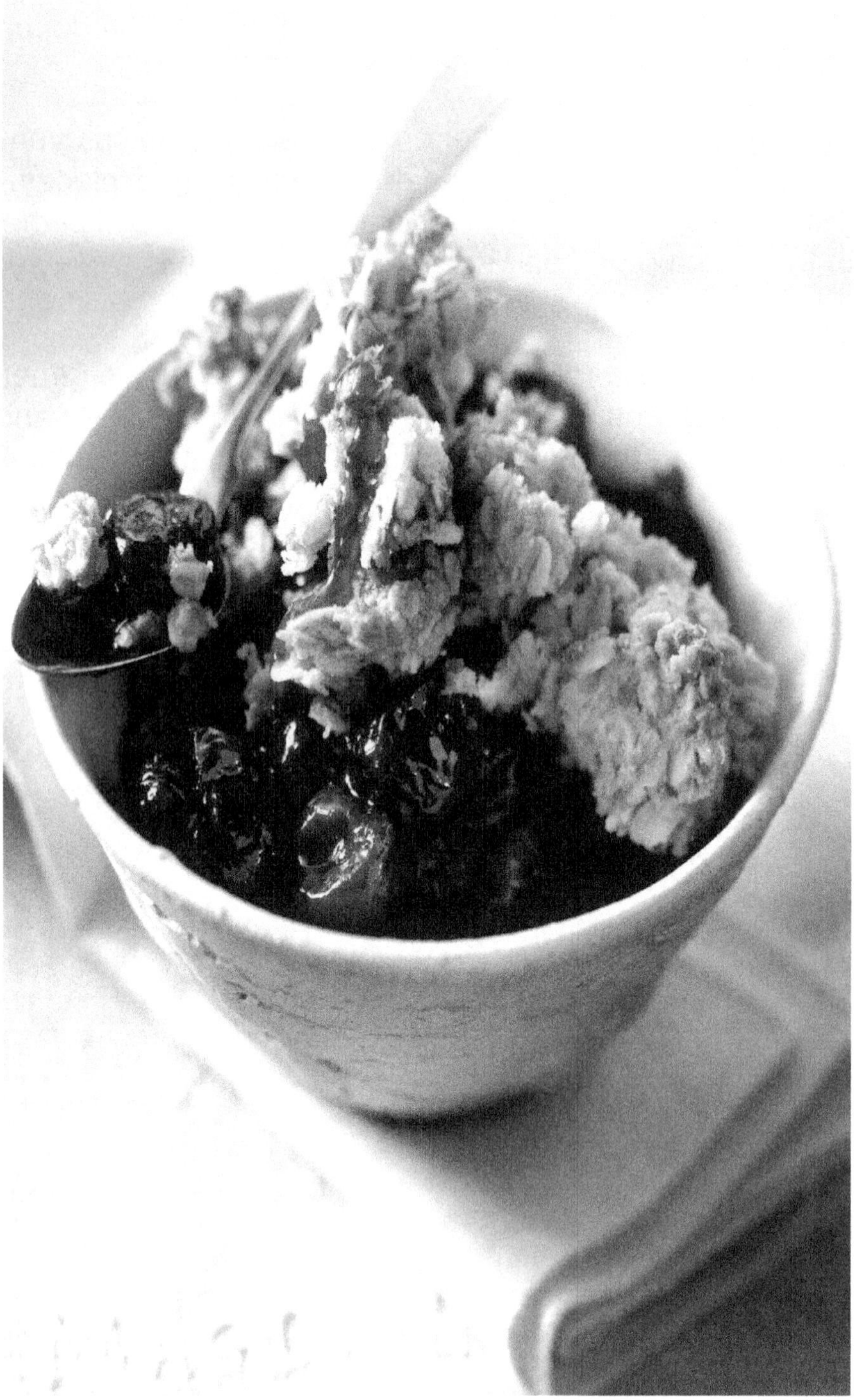

CHAPTER 9
DESSERTS

RHUBARB & STRAWBERRY CRISP

CHERRY & ALMOND CRUMBLE

CHOCOLATE BREAD PUDDING

PEAR CRISP

BRANDY BANANA FLAMBÉ

BAKED APPLES WITH CARAMEL SAUCE

ALMOND CAKE

MIXED BERRY BAKE

PEAR & CRANBERRY CRUMBLE

CLASSIC BREAD PUDDING

WHITE WINE & SPICE POACHED PEARS

RHUBARB & STRAWBERRY CRISP

SERVES 6 TO 8 PREP TIME: 20 MINUTES COOK TIME: 35 TO 40 MINUTES

A perfect blend of tart and sweet, the combination of rhubarb and strawberry makes this dessert a true palate teaser. Although rhubarb is a perennial vegetable (used as a fruit in desserts and jams), the ideal time to bake this dish is midspring through July—the stalks become tougher throughout the summer. Serve warm with vanilla ice cream for an extra-special treat.

V

6 tablespoons butter, plus extra for greasing

3 cups sliced rhubarb

3 cups sliced strawberries

¾ cup sugar

1 tablespoon cornstarch

¾ cup flour

¾ cup brown sugar

½ cup rolled oats

½ teaspoon cinnamon

1 Preheat the oven to 350°F.

2 Grease a Dutch oven with butter.

3 In a large bowl, combine the rhubarb, strawberries, sugar, and cornstarch. Place the fruit mixture in the Dutch oven.

4 Combine the flour, the brown sugar, and the remaining 6 tablespoons of butter, and use two forks to blend until the mixture resembles coarse crumbs. Add the oats and cinnamon. Mix again. Spoon the topping over the fruit mixture.

5 Cover the pot and bake for 35 to 40 minutes, or until the top is lightly browned and crisp.

INGREDIENT TIP: *Because it's extremely resistant to disease, rhubarb is one of the least sprayed or treated crops, which means that conventionally grown is almost equivalent to organic. When shopping for rhubarb, check both ends of the stalks to ensure they aren't dried out. Refrigerate and use within a few days or freeze.*

CHERRY & ALMOND CRUMBLE

SERVES 4 TO 6 PREP TIME: 20 MINUTES COOK TIME: 35 TO 40 MINUTES

This berry-and-nut crumble is not only melt-in-your mouth good, it's also a fabulous dessert to serve to a crowd with food sensitivities. Almond flour keeps it wheat-free, and if you swap out the butter for margarine, it also becomes friendly to dairy-free and vegan diets. It's perfect paired with vanilla or almond ice cream, made either with or without dairy.

V

1 cup rolled oats
¾ cup sugar, divided
1 cup almond flour
¼ teaspoon baking soda
2 pinches salt, divided
3 tablespoons butter
½ cup chopped almonds (preferably Marcona)
3 cups fresh cherries, pitted
½ teaspoon ground cinnamon

1 Preheat the oven to 350°F.

2 In a food processor, combine the oats, ¼ cup of sugar, almond flour, baking soda, and 1 pinch of salt. Pulse. Add the butter, and

pulse until combined. Mix in the chopped almonds. In a Dutch oven, spread the crumble mixture evenly.

3 In a large bowl, combine the remaining ½ cup sugar, cherries, cinnamon, and the remaining 1 pinch salt. Spread the cherry mixture on top of the crumble mixture in the Dutch oven.

4 Cover, place in the preheated oven, and bake for 35 to 40 minutes, or until the fruit is bubbly and the crust golden.

INGREDIENT TIP: *Native to Spain, Marcona almonds have become wildly popular, thanks to a growing interest in Spanish cuisine. More round and plump than the varieties we're used to seeing, they have a sweeter, more delicate taste, closer to that of almond extract—which makes them perfect for desserts and baked goods. Leftovers? These almonds make a tasty snack, a sophisticated accompaniment to a cheese plate, or a satisfying topping on salads.*

CHOCOLATE BREAD PUDDING

SERVES 4 TO 6 ■ PREP TIME: 20 MINUTES ■ COOK TIME: 1 TO 1¼ HOURS

Bread pudding is ubiquitous in many cultures, and for good reason! It's a brilliant and simple transformation of kitchen basics (bread, eggs, milk, and sugar) into mouthwatering bites. Some delectable additions—in this case, melted chocolate and the flavors of cinnamon, vanilla, and almond—convert this classic baked pudding into a truly decadent dessert.

V

Butter, for greasing

8 cups sweet bread (such as challah or brioche), cut into 1-inch cubes

¼ cup melted unsalted butter

1 cup sugar

½ cup cocoa powder

2 teaspoons cinnamon

1 teaspoon vanilla extract

½ teaspoon almond extract

¼ teaspoon salt

3 cups whole milk

4 large eggs

½ cup chocolate chips, divided

---

1 Preheat the oven to 350°F.

2 Generously grease a Dutch oven with butter.

3 Toss the bread cubes in the melted butter, and arrange in the Dutch oven. Bake for 8 to 10 minutes, or until light golden brown.

4 In a large bowl, combine the sugar, cocoa powder, cinnamon, vanilla, almond extract, and salt. Add the milk and eggs, and whisk until blended. Add the bread cubes and fold until evenly moistened. Let sit for 15 to 20 minutes, folding once or twice, until the bread cubes have absorbed most of the liquid.

5 Return half of the bread mixture to the Dutch oven. Sprinkle with ¼ cup of chocolate chips. Pour in the rest of the bread mixture, and top with the remaining ¼ cup chocolate chips.

6 Cover, return the pot to the oven, and bake for 1 to 1¼ hours, or until the top is puffed and a knife inserted near the center comes out mostly clean.

COOKING TIP: *To serve, drizzle with dulce de leche. A thick, creamy, intensely flavored spread, dulce de leche is a combination of milk and sugar that's been slowly cooked until the sugars have caramelized. It's wildly popular in Latin America—and widely available here now, too. Or you can make your own! Empty a 12-ounce can of condensed milk into your Dutch oven, and stir continuously over a medium-low heat until you can turn a cooled tablespoon upside-down without the dulce de leche falling off.*

PEAR CRISP

SERVES 6 PREP TIME: 15 MINUTES COOK TIME: 20 TO 25 MINUTES

Pear season begins when Bartletts start appearing at the market in late summer; they are soon followed by Bosc, Comice, and Anjou varieties. This recipe fills your home with the aroma of pears, combined with the heartwarming spices of cinnamon, nutmeg, and cardamom.

V **30**

6 tablespoons unsalted butter, at room temperature, plus extra for greasing

8 pears, peeled and diced into 1-inch cubes

½ teaspoon cinnamon

½ teaspoon nutmeg

½ teaspoon cardamom

½ cup brown sugar

1½ cups oats

½ cup chopped walnuts

2 tablespoons all-purpose flour

Pinch salt

1 Preheat the oven to 350°F.

2 Grease a Dutch oven with butter.

3 In a medium bowl, combine the pears, cinnamon, nutmeg, and cardamom.

4 In a separate bowl, combine the brown sugar, oats, walnuts, flour, the remaining 6 tablespoons of butter, and salt. Stir with a fork until medium-size crumbs begin to form.

5 In the bottom of the Dutch oven, place the pears. Top with the oat mixture.

6 Cover, place in the preheated oven, and bake for 20 to 25 minutes, or until the pears are tender and the crust is golden.

> **INGREDIENT TIP:** *Although Bartletts are a great choice early in the season, switch to Boscs once they hit the shelves. Because they have a firmer flesh than other pear varieties, Boscs are ideal for baking, broiling, and poaching. Plus, they have a distinctive taste that's less likely to be overwhelmed by the addition of a strong spice, such as cinnamon, nutmeg, or cardamom.*

BRANDY BANANA FLAMBÉ

SERVES 6 TO 8 PREP TIME: 10 MINUTES COOK TIME: 10 MINUTES

This is, hands down, the most impressive grand finale to a festive dinner party possible. Not only does this flambé look dramatic and taste delectable, it's incredibly easy and quick to prepare. With just four ingredients, you can end any evening on a high note.

GF V 30

5 tablespoons unsalted butter
6 bananas, thinly sliced
4 teaspoons brown sugar
¾ cup brandy (or cognac)

1 In a Dutch oven over medium-high heat, melt the butter. Sauté the bananas, sprinkling them with the brown sugar and stirring until they are slightly caramelized.

2 In a small saucepan, warm the brandy.

3 Pour the just-warmed brandy over the bananas. Strike a match, stand back, and carefully and ignite the alcohol in the pot. Shake the pot slightly so that the flame dies down, and serve directly from the Dutch oven. Top with whipped cream or ice cream.

> **COOKING TIP:** *A few simple adjustments will help perfect your flambé technique: (1) Make sure any overhead ventilation is turned off. (2) Use*

long, fireplace-length matches. (3) Stand no closer than arm's distance from the pan to ensure that your hair or clothing doesn't catch fire.

BAKED APPLES WITH CARAMEL SAUCE

SERVES 6 PREP TIME: 15 MINUTES COOK TIME: 20 TO 25 MINUTES

Nothing beats the aroma of these cinnamon-flavored baked apples. This recipe is a refreshing, light, and delicious ending to a hearty evening meal. Topped with caramel sauce, it's also the perfect way to satisfy a sweet tooth. Add a dollop of whipped cream, and watch your guests swoon.

GF **V** **30**

1 stick (8 tablespoons) butter, divided
6 apples, peeled and cored (preferably Fuji)
½ cup granulated sugar, divided
1½ teaspoons cinnamon
1¼ cups brown sugar
3 tablespoons water

1 Preheat the oven to 325°F.

2 Grease a Dutch oven with 1 tablespoon of the butter.

3 Trim a small amount off the bottom of each apple to create a flat surface. Place the apples, cut side down, in the Dutch oven. Cut 3 tablespoons of the butter in half, and place 1 piece on top of each apple.

4 In a small bowl, combine the granulated sugar and the cinnamon, and sprinkle over the apples. Cover and bake until the sugar is melted, 15 to 20 minutes. Arrange the apples on serving plates.

5 In the Dutch oven, combine the brown sugar, the remaining 8 teaspoons granulated sugar, and the water. Bring to a boil over a medium heat, and cook until thick, about 5 minutes, stirring often. Whisk in the remaining butter. Drizzle the caramel sauce over each apple.

> **INGREDIENT TIP:** *Not all apples are created equal. Fuji apples are one of the sweetest varieties. Named after Mount Fuji in Japan, they were developed in the late 1930s by blending two classic American varieties—Red Delicious and Virginia Ralls Janet. Fujis are also great storing apples, so they're available year-round.*

ALMOND CAKE

SERVES 6 TO 8 PREP TIME: 10 MINUTES COOK TIME: 30 MINUTES

Moist, delicious, and a near-universal palate pleaser, almond cake is a classic dish to round out any meal, at any time of year. It's simple to make and versatile. Serve it with a dusting of powdered sugar, top it with toasted almond slices, or garnish it with a medley of juicy berries.

V **30**

- 8 tablespoons unsalted butter, at room temperature, plus extra for greasing
- 7 ounces almond paste
- 3 large eggs
- 1 tablespoon rum or amaretto
- 2 drops almond extract
- 1/3 cup all-purpose flour
- 1/2 teaspoon baking powder

1 Preheat the oven to 350°F.

2 Grease a Dutch oven with butter.

3 In a bowl, combine the almond paste, the remaining 8 tablespoons butter, the eggs, rum, and almond extract, and blend together, using a spatula.

4 Fold the flour and the baking powder into the cake batter. Spoon into the Dutch oven.

5 Cover, place the pot in the preheated oven, and bake for 30 minutes, or until the top of the cake is golden and a knife inserted into the center comes out almost clean.

COOKING TIP: *For a berry-topped treat, brush the top of the cake with a mixture of 1 tablespoon sugar and 1 tablespoon warm water. Use 1 cup of lightly sugared berries (we love a mix of raspberries, blueberries, and blackberries) to pave the top of the cake. Top each serving with a dollop of whipped cream that includes a dash of almond extract.*

MIXED BERRY BAKE

SERVES 4 TO 6 PREP TIME: 10 MINUTES COOK TIME: 50 MINUTES

This recipe is a variation of the French clafoutis, which is a warm, thick dessert of cherries baked in a flanlike batter. Here, we've used mixed berries to impart a burst-in-your-mouth juiciness. Serve with a dusting of powdered sugar and a dollop of fresh cream.

V

Butter, for greasing
3 eggs
1 cup milk
¼ cup heavy cream
½ cup flour
1 teaspoon vanilla extract
½ cup sugar
2 cups mixed berries

1 Preheat the oven to 350°F.

2 Grease a Dutch oven with butter.

3 In a stand mixer, combine the eggs, milk, cream, flour, vanilla, and sugar, and blend on high for 30 seconds.

4 Pour 1 cup of batter into the Dutch oven. Cover, place in the preheated oven, and bake for 5 to 7 minutes.

5 Remove from the oven and arrange the berries on top. Pour the remaining batter over the fruit.

6 Return to the oven, and bake for 45 minutes, or until golden and a knife inserted in the center comes out almost clean.

> **SUBSTITUTION TIP:** *This dish can be reinvented time and again by substituting your choice of fresh fruit (or, if you're stuck, frozen). A particularly delightful variation is peach. Substitute 2 medium peaches, peeled and thinly sliced, for the mixed berries.*

PEAR & CRANBERRY CRUMBLE

SERVES 6 TO 8 PREP TIME: 20 MINUTES COOK TIME: 45 MINUTES

Fall is the prime season for cranberries, which reach their peak flavor and color from mid-September through mid-November. But you can bake this tart but oh-so-sweet dish any time of year by swapping in frozen berries. Notes of maple syrup, cinnamon, and nutmeg contribute a hint of spicy warmth, while walnuts add to the rich, nutty texture. Serve with vanilla ice cream!

V

5 large pears, peeled, cored, and sliced

1 pound fresh or frozen cranberries

2 tablespoons maple syrup

⅓ cup sugar

½ teaspoon cinnamon, divided

¼ teaspoon nutmeg

1 cup rolled oats

⅔ cup brown sugar

1 stick plus 2 tablespoons butter, cut into ½-inch pieces

½ cup all-purpose flour

½ cup chopped walnuts

1 Preheat the oven to 350°F.

2 In a Dutch oven, combine the pears and cranberries, and drizzle them with the maple syrup. Add the sugar, ¼ teaspoon of cinnamon, and nutmeg. Toss together until well mixed.

3 In a bowl, combine the oats, brown sugar, butter, flour, the remaining ¼ teaspoon of cinnamon, and chopped walnuts. Use your fingertips to blend coarsely. Sprinkle the oat mixture over the fruit and pat down lightly.

4 Cover, place the pot in the preheated oven, and bake for about 45 minutes, until the pears are tender and the crust is golden.

> **NUTRITION TIP:** *Most cranberries are water harvested, meaning they're grown in bogs and the berries float on the surface of the water. Research shows this increased exposure to natural sunlight not only increases the phytonutrients that give the cranberry its amazing red color, it also boosts its antioxidant and anti-inflammatory properties, making the cranberry one super-healthy fruit.*

CLASSIC BREAD PUDDING

SERVES 6 TO 8 ▪ PREP TIME: 30 MINUTES ▪ COOK TIME: 1 HOUR

This dessert is the perfect choice for the day when the pantry is bare. All you need is bread, eggs, milk, and sugar. Although sweet bread is ideal, just about any bread past its prime will do. Drizzle each dish with warmed caramel syrup (find it in the ice cream topping section of your supermarket), and your family will be clamoring for seconds.

V

Butter, for greasing

- 9 to 10 cups bread (ideally a sweet bread, such as challah or brioche), diced into 1-inch cubes
- 3 eggs, lightly beaten
- 4 cups milk
- ½ cup sugar
- 1 teaspoon vanilla extract
- ¼ teaspoon salt

1 Heat the oven to 325°F.

2 Grease a Dutch oven with butter, and add the bread cubes.

3 In a large bowl, combine the eggs, milk, sugar, vanilla, and salt. Pour the egg mixture over the bread cubes. Using the back of a wooden spoon, press down lightly to moisten the bread. Let sit for

15 to 20 minutes, folding the mixture once or twice, until the bread cubes have absorbed most of the liquid.

4 Cover the pot, place in the heated oven, and cook for 1 hour, or until golden brown.

> **SUBSTITUTION TIP:** Challah is the traditional Jewish sabbath bread made with yeast and eggs. It is wonderfully soft and rich, which makes it an ideal choice for bread pudding. Another excellent, even richer, option is French-style brioche, which typically contains butter as well as eggs. Alternative options include Portuguese sweet bread, Hawaiian sweet bread, or croissants. But if you're in a pinch, just about any type of bread will do nicely.

WHITE WINE & SPICE POACHED PEARS

SERVES 4 PREP TIME: 10 MINUTES COOK TIME: 30 MINUTES

While this recipe calls for Riesling wine, you can use any fruity white, such as Pinot Grigio or Muscat. If you can find one, choose a German Auslese or Spatlese Riesling, which has a nice balance of sweetness and acidity that complement the pears and the spices.

V

1 750 mL bottle Riesling

1 teaspoon whole cloves

1 teaspoon cardamom pods

2 cinnamon sticks

2 strips orange peel, ½ inch wide by 2 inches long

4 pears, stems and peels removed, cut in half

1 In a large Dutch oven, bring the Riesling, cloves, cardamom, cinnamon, and orange peel to a simmer over medium-high heat.

2 Add the pears. Put a plate over the top of them as a weight to keep them submerged in the liquid.

3 Reduce the heat to medium-low. Simmer until the pears are tender, about 25 minutes.

4 Serve the pears with the poaching liquid (minus the spices and orange peel) spooned over the top.

COOKING TIP: *Remove the orange peel using a peeler. Be sure to get only the orange part of the peel, leaving the bitter white part (the pith) on the orange.*

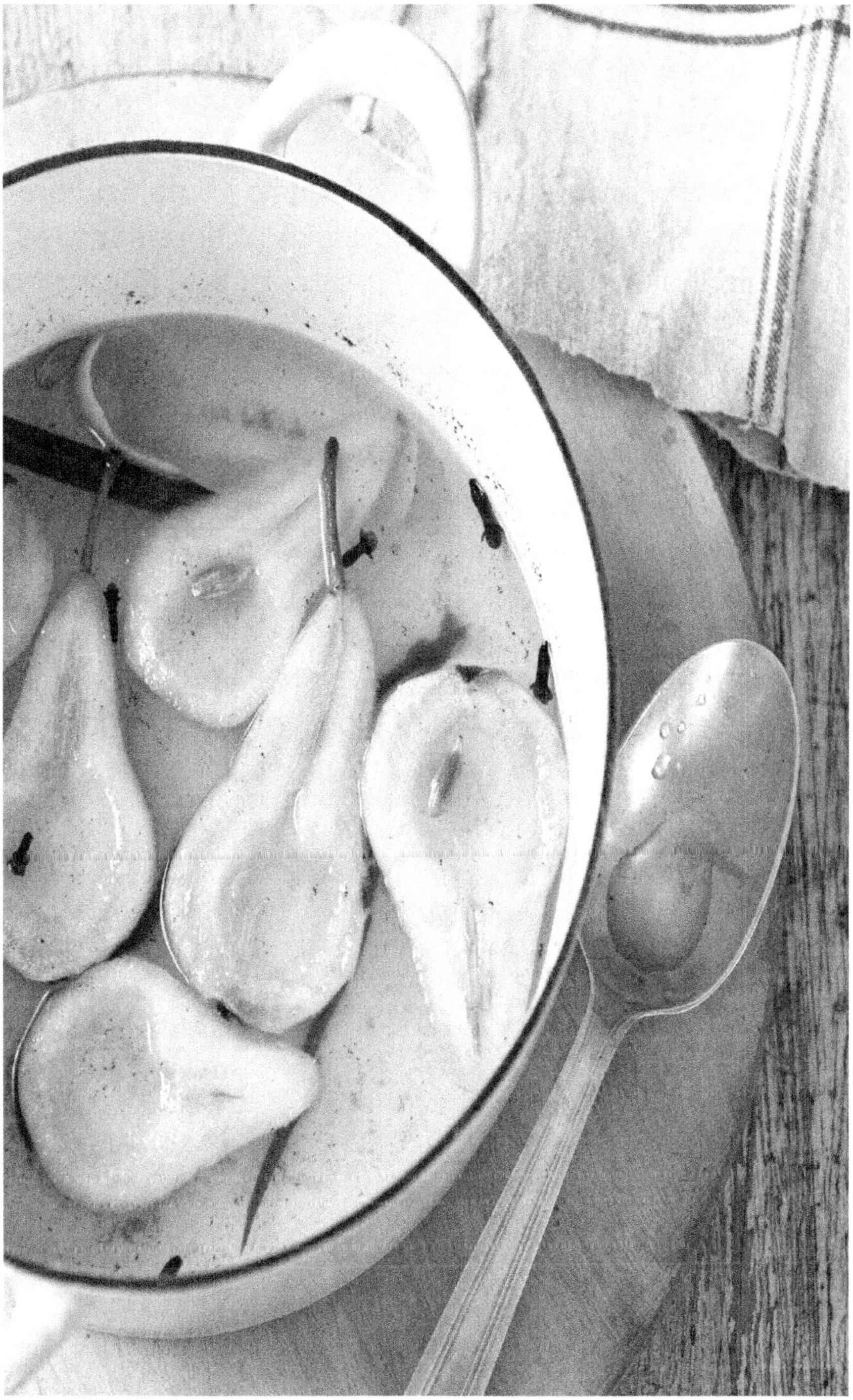

APPENDIX A
The Dirty Dozen & Clean Fifteen

A nonprofit and environmental watchdog organization called Environmental Working Group (EWG) looks at data supplied by the US Department of Agriculture (USDA) and the Food and Drug Administration (FDA) about pesticide residues. Each year it compiles a list of the best and worst pesticide loads found in commercial crops. You can use these lists to decide which fruits and vegetables to buy organic to minimize your exposure to pesticides and which produce is considered safe enough to buy conventionally. This does not mean they are pesticide-free, though, so wash these fruits and vegetables thoroughly.

These lists change every year, so make sure you look up the most recent one before you fill your shopping cart. You'll find the most recent lists as well as a guide to pesticides in produce at EWG.org/FoodNews.

2015 DIRTY DOZEN

Apples
Celery
Cherry tomatoes
Cucumbers
Grapes
Nectarines (imported)
Peaches
Potatoes
Snap peas (imported)
Spinach

Strawberries
Sweet bell peppers

In addition to the dirty dozen, the EWG added two produce contaminated with highly toxic organo-phosphate insecticides:

Kale/Collard greens
Hot peppers

2015 CLEAN FIFTEEN

Asparagus
Avocados
Cabbage
Cantaloupes (domestic)
Cauliflower
Eggplants
Grapefruits
Kiwis
Mangoes
Onions
Papayas
Pineapples
Sweet corn
Sweet peas (frozen)
Sweet potatoes

APPENDIX B
Measurement Conversions

VOLUME EQUIVALENTS (LIQUID)

US STANDARD	US STANDARD (OUNCES)	METRIC (APPROXIMATE)
2 tablespoons	1 fl. oz.	30 mL
¼ cup	2 fl. oz.	60 mL
½ cup	4 fl. oz.	120 mL
1 cup	8 fl. oz.	240 mL
1½ cups	12 fl. oz.	355 mL
2 cups or 1 pint	16 fl. oz.	475 mL
4 cups or 1 quart	32 fl. oz.	1 L
1 gallon	128 fl. oz.	4 L

VOLUME EQUIVALENTS (DRY)

US STANDARD	METRIC (APPROXIMATE)
1/8 teaspoon	0.5 mL
1/4 teaspoon	1 mL
1/2 teaspoon	2 mL
3/4 teaspoon	4 mL
1 teaspoon	5 mL
1 tablespoon	15 mL
1/4 cup	59 mL
1/3 cup	79 mL
1/2 cup	118 mL
2/3 cup	156 mL
3/4 cup	177 mL
1 cup	235 mL
2 cups or 1 pint	475 mL
3 cups	700 mL
4 cups or 1 quart	1 L

OVEN TEMPERATURES

FAHRENHEIT (F)	CELSIUS (C) (APPROXIMATE)
250°	120°
300°	150°
325°	165°
350°	180°
375°	190°
400°	200°
425°	220°
450°	230°

WEIGHT EQUIVALENTS

US STANDARD	METRIC (APPROXIMATE)
½ ounce	15 g
1 ounce	30 g
2 ounces	60 g
4 ounces	115 g
8 ounces	225 g
12 ounces	340 g
16 ounces or 1 pound	455 g

Printed in Great Britain
by Amazon